"Inspired and inspiring. This gentle and tender gem of a book—which includes numerous easy-to-follow 'try this!' exercises specifically designed to tame the 'reacting brain'—will prove to be an invaluable treasure trove for all teens committed to letting go of their anxiety and worry."

—**Martha Stark, MD**, faculty, Harvard Medical School

"Bernstein's book is an invaluable resource for both teens and parents. He distills complex issues with a sensitivity born of experience, offering sage advice as well as practical exercises, to help ease worry and anxiety during these years of intense change. Superbly researched and deeply insightful, every sentence rings true."

—**Leah Kaminsky**, physician; author and winner of the Voss Literary Prize for *The Waiting Room*

"I am very excited about Jeff Bernstein's new book, because it fills a critical gap in an area that has been begging for mindful attention. This book is written in a voice that teenagers can easily relate to.… Mindfulness, as Bernstein points out, is not a panacea, but it is a tool. The mind-body connection that Bernstein discusses in the book is quite important to kids in their formative teen years. As a public school superintendent, I understand that mindfulness can stop the cycle of a worried mind and stressed body by changing how you respond.… I am looking forward, with eager anticipation, to sharing this book with those who need it most: kids and those who spend lots of time with them. Thank you, Dr. Jeff!"

—**Ivan Katz**, superintendent of schools for the Fallsburg Central School District in Fallsburg, NY

"Chock-full of practical, helpful, and fun ideas for transforming your relationship with worry now, and for the rest of your life."

—**Christopher Willard, PsyD**, author of *Mindfulness for Teen Anxiety*, and coauthor of *Mindfulness for Teen Depression*; Cambridge Health Alliance/Harvard Medical School

"If you are looking for a practical, relatable, and easy-to-read book that will teach your teen how to cope with stress and anxiety, *this is it!* Bernstein's latest book is a wonderful and comprehensive new resource for teens that teaches basic mindfulness strategies and shows how they can be applied to various types of common adolescent struggles. As a clinical child psychologist, I will definitely be recommending this book to my anxious teen patients."

—**Stephanie Margolese, PhD**, clinical psychologist, and author of *Sam's Big Secret* and *When Monkey Lost His Smile*

"With his easy and accessible tone, Bernstein shares his experiences working with teen clients on how mindfulness has helped them let go of worry and gain inner resources. This book is filled with mindfulness practices specific to the very situations that most often cause teens to worry—school pressures, family relationships, body image, and social dynamics. This is a great book for any teen who has ever worried—or will ever worry. In other words, a great resource for all teens!"

—**Karen Bluth, PhD**, author of *The Self-Compassion Workbook for Teens*, and assistant professor at the University of North Carolina School of Medicine

"*Mindfulness for Teen Worry* provides a treasure trove of mindfulness-based practices to kick worries to the curb. Teens today are managing so much with social media and other pressures, that worrying is a natural and normal response. Bernstein shows teens a positive and healthy way out of worrying. I wish I had this resource myself when I was a teen!"

> —**Gina M. Biegel, MA, LMFT**, psychotherapist; author of *The Stress Reduction Workbook for Teens*, *Be Mindful and Stress Less*, and *Be Mindful Card Deck for Teens*; and founder of the Mindfulness-Based Stress Reduction for Teens (MBSR-T) and Stressed Teens programs

"Our teens are more stressed than ever before. Easy to read, Bernstein's book gives teens simple, practical tools to transform stress into positive energy. From deep experience with teens, Bernstein offers insight and a path with clear structure using brief exercises in awareness, breathing, and visualization to help cope with external conflict, mixed emotions, and everyday pressures. A must-read for teens, parents, and teachers."

> —**Richard P. Brown, MD**, associate clinical professor in psychiatry at Columbia University College of Physicians and Surgeons, and coauthor of *The Healing Power of the Breath*

"Jeff Bernstein's book on teen worry is superb: equal parts educational and inspirational. A must-read for teenagers and everyone in their lives—parents and therapists alike!"

> —**Shannon L. Delaney, MD, MA**, child and adolescent psychiatrist on the faculty of Columbia University Medical Center

the *i n s t a n t   h e l p*
s o l u t i o n s   s e r i e s

Young people today need mental health resources more than ever. That's why New Harbinger created the **Instant Help Solutions Series** especially for teens. Written by leading psychologists, physicians, and professionals, these evidence-based self-help books offer practical tips and strategies for dealing with a variety of mental health issues and life challenges teens face, such as depression, anxiety, bullying, eating disorders, trauma, and self-esteem problems.

Studies have shown that young people who learn healthy coping skills early on are better able to navigate problems later in life. Engaging and easy-to-use, these books provide teens with the tools they need to thrive—at home, at school, and on into adulthood.

This series is part of the **New Harbinger Instant Help Books** imprint, founded by renowned child psychologist Lawrence Shapiro. For a complete list of books in this series, visit newharbinger.com.

mindfulness

for **teen worry**

quick & **easy**
strategies to **let go** of
anxiety, worry
& **stress**

JEFFREY BERNSTEIN, PhD

Instant Help Books
An Imprint of New Harbinger Publications, Inc.

Publisher's Note

Distributed in Canada by Raincoast Books

Copyright © 2017 by Jeffrey Bernstein
     Instant Help Books
     An imprint of New Harbinger Publications, Inc.
     5674 Shattuck Avenue
     Oakland, CA 94609
     www.newharbinger.com

The exercises "Gaining Acceptance through Self-Compassion" and "Self-Acceptance Hug for Self-Compassion" are adapted with permission from the work of Kristin Neff.

Cover design by Amy Shoup

Acquired by Elizabeth Hollis Hansen

Edited by Will DeRooy

All Rights Reserved

Library of Congress Cataloging-in-Publication Data

21 20 19

10 9 8 7 6 5 4 3 2

To Marina, the love of my life, for broadening my world by inspiring me to keep learning and growing.

To my lovable children, Alissa, Sam, and Gabby, for the valuable lessons you each taught me through your teen years and the lessons you continue to teach me as adults.

And to all my teen clients, for sharing with me your personal stories of resilience and mindful wisdom.

Contents

Introduction

This book is for every teen who worries. In other words, this book is for almost every teen, because worry is a very common problem for both male and female adolescents. As a teen, you frequently face new situations and pursue different and more challenging goals as a part of growing up. What with school demands, social pressures, physical changes, and family stress, you may have some big-time worries on your plate.

I've been a child and teen psychologist for more than thirty years, and my teenage clients tell me that worrying makes them feel weighed down, distracted, stressed out, and even miserable.

Some teens tell me they just can't stop worrying or that their worrying keeps bad things from happening. Since you're reading this book, you may feel the same way. But you can soon learn to see your worries in a different way and not feel so weighed down by them. This different way of seeing is based on some simple mindfulness practices. Teens tell me this "mindfulness stuff" really works, helping them to feel less uptight and even happier. Mindfulness can help you effectively manage your worries both now and later—as you enter into college, the working world, or even parenthood—leading to more opportunities and a more fulfilling, meaningful life.

How Can Mindfulness Help You Worry Less?

As a teen in this fast-paced digital age, you are facing more pressures and worries than any generation that came before you. Mindfulness helps you notice what is going on inside your mind, inside your body, and in the world around you, shifting your focus away from troublesome thoughts buzzing around in your head.

Practicing mindfulness will very likely change your life for the better. I am really excited to share with you the same mindfulness skills that have worked for the more than three thousand teens I have counseled.

Mindfulness Is Easy to Learn

The capacity for mindfulness is already within you. You don't have to go to the top of a mountain or deep in the woods to practice mindfulness. You can do it just about anywhere you are. Doing just a few minutes of mindfulness exercises a day, or even a few times a week, and seeing yourself and the world around you in a mindful way will result in your worries being less frequent and less intense. Your willingness, patience, imagination, attention, and breath are the only things you need to make mindfulness work for you for the rest of your life.

How to Get the Most from This Book

Reading this book will not stop you from ever worrying again. But once you begin to use mindfulness skills, you will worry less intensely and less often. The teens I teach mindfulness to frequently tell me that simply knowing how to manage their worries leaves them feeling less anxious and helps them feel happier, too!

In the first part of this book (chapters 1 to 5), you will learn why you worry and how anxiety can turn you into your own worst enemy. You'll learn that you are not in control of what thoughts pop into your head. Yet accepting this reality will, perhaps surprisingly, help you have fewer worries. Quick, easy-to-learn, interesting exercises will help you notice your breath, your thoughts, your feelings, your bodily sensations, your senses, and what's happening around you in a different, special way.

The second part of this book (chapters 6 to 9) will help you use mindfulness to deal with the four biggest areas of worries that most teens struggle with: school pressures, social concerns and relationship problems, body-image issues, and family conflicts.

The third and final part (chapter 10 and the appendix) will suggest some valuable strategies you can use to make mindfulness a lifelong skill. You will also learn about getting mental health support in case you experience severe anxiety.

Throughout this book are sections entitled "Teens in Their Own Words." The quotes in these sections reflect what teens (although their names have been changed, to protect their confidentiality) have expressed to me in my counseling practice. Every chapter also includes exercises (under the heading "Try This!") with hands-on activities and exercises to give you simple but highly effective mindfulness skills. Audio versions of many of these exercises are available for download at this book's New

Harbinger Publications website, http://www.newharbinger.com/39812. (See the very back of this book for more details.)

I am excited for you to learn how awesome mindfulness is for managing your worries. I'm confident that the mindfulness skills you gain from this book can help you feel calmer and happier throughout your life. Go forward with an open mind and with non-judgmental curiosity as you learn these cool new ways to be less worried.

PART 1

Moving Out of Worry Wasteland with Mindfulness

chapter 1

why you get stuck in worry wasteland

I am an old man and have known a great many troubles, but most of them have never happened.

—Mark Twain

It has been said that the average person has about 48.6 thoughts per minute. If this is true, it means that people have about 50,000 to 70,000 thoughts per day.

Whoa. That's a huge amount of thoughts bouncing around in your brain! Given that you're reading this book, it's more than likely that many of those thoughts consist of worries. Whereas other thoughts seem to come and go, those worries can stick around until it feels as though your head is full of them.

Worries are thoughts, images, and emotions of a negative nature meant to help you avoid anticipated potential threats. Some people tend to worry more than others, and it is not clear whether this is due to genetics, environmental factors, or people's personalities. People sometimes worry about things that happened in the past, but most of the time, especially for teens, worries are thoughts about what might happen in the future. Even though worries are meant to help you, they often waste your time and energy because the vast majority of things you worry about often don't end up happening or, if they do, they don't turn out to be as bad as your worried mind led you to believe.

How many times a day would you say you feel worried? Worry can take many forms. You probably worry more often than you realize. For example, all the following feelings point to a worried state of mind.

fear	concerned	uptight
overwhelmed	jittery	triggered
nervous	alarmed	butterflies
panicked	freaking out	stressed out
uneasy	restless	edgy

Feeling as though your thoughts are racing, or your mind is moving a mile a minute, is also an indicator of worry.

Why Are You Worried?

At this time in your life, your entire body is going through huge changes thanks to puberty (I'll spare you the embarrassment of getting into specifics—for now). Hopefully in health class you learned what to expect, but still you may be feeling self-conscious and insecure, or at least conflicted, about some or all of those changes.

In addition, now that you're in middle school or high school, you'll face greater academic challenges than ever before. In all likelihood, you have a demanding schedule of classes, homework, and extracurricular activities. You may wonder whether you're putting in enough effort, whether you'll do well, and whether you can successfully balance school with your other responsibilities. Keeping up with activities and other interests, although they may be fun, can be a significant source of stress and worry.

And what about the pressure to fit in? Because it can be hard to tell whether and how much your peers like you or approve of you, your social life may feel like a minefield. Teens tell me of sometimes feeling as though if they make one bad step, they'll be rejected or teased. Even their friends may say or do things that seem to shut them out, leaving them wondering what they did wrong. And the world of social media can be just as tough to navigate as real life.

Last but not least, things can be frustrating at home. Your parents love you and care about you, but they may struggle to really understand the demands in your life (compared to what it was like when they were your age). You may have the impression that they're always judging you even though they're likely trying hard to be supportive. If you have a brother or sister, you're likely no stranger to arguments, bickering over who gets what, and even being downright hostile toward each other.

So, between all the physical changes and pressures buzzing inside you and around you, it's understandable if you're worried about a lot of things right now. Do you ever have so many worries that it's hard for you to catch a break from your anxiety? It may feel as though there's no escape from the pressures in your life—that there's nothing else in sight. No matter which way your mind turns, big-time worries pop up in front of you. This feeling doesn't last forever, but while it does—while you're stuck in what I call "worry wasteland"—you're just spinning your wheels, hopelessly wishing for your anxieties to just magically disappear. One of my clients, James, age fifteen, summed up how he felt during his trips to worry wasteland when he said: "Dr. Jeff, some days I wish I could be a kid in elementary school again. There sure would be fewer things to worry about!"

Here are some examples of things that teens say they worry about. Can you relate to any of these worries?

Teens in Their Own Words

"I worry that people think I'm too weird to fit in."
—Luke, age thirteen

"I am freaking out; I think I bombed that test."
—Tony, age fourteen

"I'm really paranoid that other kids are going to say bad things about me when they find out that he dumped me."
—Tamika, age fifteen

"What if they think I look ugly? I can't go to the dance being fat and with my skin looking like this." —Jessica, age sixteen

"I'm really worried that I did something to hurt my best friend's feelings and that I may mess up future friendships in college."
—Allison, age eighteen

To begin to deal with your worries, and get out of worry wasteland, you first need to understand what causes them.

Understanding Your Brain

There is a "hands on," so to speak, way to understand the brain. The "hand model of the brain" developed by Dr. Daniel Siegel helps you grasp what goes on inside your brain, including when you visit worry wasteland. Teens tell me that by seeing how their brain works, it is easier for them to manage their worries.

Bend your left elbow and hold your left hand in front of you at eye level. Now make a fist (with your thumb on the inside of your palm), keeping it at eye level (have no fear, I'm not going to ask you to punch yourself as a new trick to stop worrying). Keep your hand in place as you read on.

Your "Primitive Brain" or "Reacting Brain"

Your wrist represents your spinal cord, and as it comes up to your skull it becomes your brain stem. This lower area, where your spinal cord meets the base of your skull, houses what's called the hindbrain. The hindbrain is the most basic and, evolutionarily speaking, the oldest part of the brain. (If you don't believe in evolution, this part of the brain is something that even simple creatures such as lizards have.) It controls breathing, heart rate, and blood pressure, and gives you your survival instincts. Now look at your thumb. Your thumb represents the limbic system, which sits on top of the hindbrain.

The limbic system is the place where we hold, store, and integrate memories of fears and where we experience other emotions. The amygdala, an almond-shaped set of brain cells in this region, allows us to react quickly to things we feel threatened by or are afraid of.

11

The limbic system and hindbrain work together to initiate the "fight, flight, or freeze" response that is so important to our basic survival. If—as early humans sometimes did—you suddenly meet a fierce-looking tiger, only one thing matters to your life in that instant: your ability to fight it, to run away from it, or to play dead in the hopes that it ignores you. As you no doubt realize, your chances of running into a tiger in this day and age are super slim. Yet, thanks to genes you inherited from your prehistoric ancestors, your "primitive brain" is wired to be on the lookout for tigers and other scary beasts—or simply the things that make you the most nervous—and to react as if your life depends on being ready to fight, flee, or freeze. If you're like most teens, in your day-to-day routine there *are* no potentially fatal threats lurking around corners. So instead you dread getting slammed with a ton of homework, feeling awkward or insecure around a new group of people, or letting your secret crush see you on a bad hair day, as though *these* things might be just as disastrous to your health, well-being, or hopes for the future. Pretty unrealistic, right?

Your "Thinking Brain"

Still looking at your hand? Good. Your fingers represent the top and front part of your brain. This is your cortex, the evolutionarily newer, higher part of the brain. (If you don't believe in evolution, this part of the brain is much more advanced in humans than in cats, dogs, and other animals.) Your cortex allows you to perceive the outside world and to think and reason. It also regulates the feelings in your lower brain—when your lower brain raises an alarm, your cortex can tell it, "Stay calm" or, "It's going to be okay."

When you are feeling uncertain about school pressures, peer or family stress, or your secret crush, especially if you are tired or someone pushes one of your emotional buttons, you can end up "flipping your lid" (lift up your fingers from resting on your thumb to see a literal representation of "flipping your lid"). When this happens, the crucial thinking and reasoning frontal part of your brain goes "off-line." This is also known as "freaking out," "flipping out," or "losing it." What all this means is that if you are really feeling stressed, scared, or angry, your cortex—your "thinking brain" loses the ability to control your knee-jerk emotional and physical reactions. At those times, your worries really get the best of you, and you may try to (physically or verbally) resist or run away from whatever is making you feel so upset. You may end up saying or doing things you later regret. Or you may freeze—for example, you find yourself unable to speak or to begin working on something you need to get done. (After you've read this book, hopefully these sorts of things will happen less often.)

Worrying Can Help and Even Save You...

As you probably know, being alert, without "flipping your lid," can be really important. If you get worried about getting into a car with a driver who is high, your brain is warning you and with good reason—the driver and you could crash. If you are walking in a crime-ridden area in the middle of the night, that warning message from this reacting part of your brain—that feeling of worry—is important for you to stay safe. Getting worried can prompt you to take precautions if there's a real danger lurking in the shadows.

Even in less dire situations, challenges that can trigger worrying are a part of life. Preparing for tests, meeting new people, speaking in public, going on a date, and competing in sports can make you feel apprehensive or uneasy. If your brain is telling you to study, it is for a good reason: if you don't study, then you're probably not going to do too well. In fact, when you're studying for a test, a little anxiety can make you want to study hard so you learn the material and get a decent grade. Similarly, if you're about to participate in a wrestling tournament, field hockey game, piano recital, or dance recital, it makes sense to have the jitters, because you need to stay aware of the demands of the situation.

...But Most Worries Are Useless, Unhelpful Alerts

Worrying can be helpful when it spurs you to take action or solve a problem, as in the preceding examples. However, apart from these obvious situations where worry might be warranted, very often it is not. Your "primitive brain" (your hindbrain and limbic system) can flood you with needless worries (and most are needless, aren't they?), getting you worked up over things that have not even happened yet.

A very common, annoying worry pattern is "What if" thoughts. As Wes's example shows, those "What ifs" can really make mountains out of molehills!

Teens in Their Own Words

"I had this big test coming up. I thought I was all set, but then some kids were talking about it in the cafeteria and I started to worry. But I wasn't just worried about failing the test—I was also thinking What if I don't get into college? What if my family and friends think I am a loser? and What if I end up on the street because I can't even get a job? Then I started to worry What if I keep dwelling on what ifs?!" —Wes, age sixteen

We'll come back to Wes in chapter 2 and later to explain how we found his way out of worry wasteland. For now, can you relate to Wes's example of being stuck in "What if" thoughts? Check out this activity to manage your "What ifs."

try this! Exploring Your "What Ifs"

Close your eyes and reflect on the "What ifs" that you have struggled with in the past and those that still come into your mind. Make a list of these "What ifs." Reflect on each "What if?" and think about how it gets in your way.

Afterward, ask yourself whether it was it helpful to write out your "What ifs." Can you see how these "What ifs" can really get your mind racing?

The good news is that most of the time in life, bad stuff—our "What ifs"—does not happen. So why, then, do we still waste so much time worrying?

Put another way, no one likes the way frequent worrying makes them feel, so why can worries seem so difficult and tricky to control? The answers lie in your beliefs—both negative and positive—about worrying. Many teens tell me that, beyond occasional jitters, their excessive worrying helps them believe that stressful problems will turn out okay. Some teens have even told me that they believe worrying shows others that they are a caring and conscientious person. It's tough to break the worry habit if you believe that your worrying protects you or that it makes you a "good" person. In order to manage your worries for the long haul, it helps to see that these beliefs that worrying serves a positive purpose are not true. In fact, worrying just leads to more stress. One teen described worrying to me as "a huge amount of weight on my shoulders." Let's take a look at what that can mean.

How Worrying Weighs You Down

Teens like the ones quoted earlier tell me about the many ways that worrying interferes with their lives. Excessive worry can make it hard for you to concentrate in class, get homework and school projects done, enjoy time with friends, and feel good about yourself. Following are some reasons why.

Worrying Can Make Things Worse

Dawn, a fifteen-year-old client of mine, said to me, "Dr. Jeff, I am realizing that when I worry about someone or something, I am just living in doubt with zero benefits." In Dawn's case, she was worried that a friend was going to reject her. She started to mentally replay and analyze every interaction they had. Then she called a mutual friend and discussed the issue with her. Her friend then leaked Dawn's concerns to other friends; all this did was create gossip and negative energy.

Dawn also found that her worries made things worse because they would come out sideways. She told me: "Sometimes when I get worried I also get distant. One of my friends thought I didn't care about something important going on in her life. I really did care, but I guess I seemed kind of self-absorbed because I was busy worrying about my own stuff."

Worrying Gets in Your Way

The two most important skills we need for success in life are the ability to calm ourselves down and the ability to solve problems. Teens often share with me that worrying can really get in the way of both of these crucial coping skills. When you get really worked up with worries, you don't have enough energy left for creative solutions.

One time, Craig, a high-school freshman I worked with, was worried about a book report he needed to write. He was plagued by thoughts such as whatever he wrote wouldn't be as good as the other kids' book reports. He realized that the more he worried about it, the further he was from getting it done. That was because his thoughts that his work would not be good enough made it hard for him to calm down so that he could create an outline and actually begin the writing process. Craig felt very happy and greatly relieved by being able to start and complete this assignment using the very same skills that you will be learning in this book.

Worrying Is Wasted Energy

In my almost thirty years of counseling teens, none have told me that having their head filled with worries helped them have a more productive day! Worrying is fruitless because it robs you of time that you could be using to relax or get things done. This is because worries are negative thoughts, images, and emotions about things you find threatening. Focusing on threats, which usually are not even going to happen, keeps you from getting helpful things done.

try this! Seeing How Worries Are Wasted Energy

Think of times in your life when your worrying didn't provide you with the benefits you hoped it would, such as safety or a feeling of control. Write them down on a piece of paper, and then reflect on the following questions:

- How does worrying waste energy?

- What things do you often miss out on when you waste time worrying?

- What are some enjoyable things you could be doing instead of worrying?

Worrying Can Make You Physically Ill

In order to survive, your prehistoric ancestors had to decide whether to fight, run, or freeze when facing a saber-toothed tiger. This "fight, flight, or freeze" response, which is a function of your "reacting brain," causes your body's nervous system to release stress hormones. These hormones get you ready for action, which can be tremendously helpful in the short term. Over the long term, however, consistently high levels of stress hormones (one result of excessive worry) can negatively affect your nervous system, your organs, and your glands. The more stressed your body becomes, the worse you can feel. I often see teens whose out-of-control worrying leads to headaches, stomachaches, sleep issues, physical illnesses, and depression. (We'll explore physical symptoms and ways to alleviate them in chapter 5.)

Worry vs. Anxiety Disorders

All teens feel worried at times. This book focuses on normal, manageable worries, rather than severe, persistent worries that cross the line to become an ongoing mental health problem. How do you tell the difference between the two—where is the line? Well, worry creates mild to moderate emotional distress, whereas anxiety disorders tend to create severe emotional distress, to the point of not being able to function. As we will discuss, common teen worries can bring on some of the same physical symptoms as anxiety disorders, but to a much lesser and more manageable degree.

Teens sometimes ask me with great concern if they have an anxiety disorder. The term "anxiety disorder" means that your worrying has become so extreme that it can be hard to make it through the day and even lead a normal life. This type of disorder is considered very serious compared to the common bouts of worry that every teen struggles with from time to time. If you have an anxiety disorder, your worries and fears are higher than normal and may feel almost never-ending. Some teens with anxiety disorders worry so intensely that they avoid going to school or even being out in public for fear that something bad will happen. Although there are several kinds of anxiety disorders, they all have some common symptoms. These include feelings of panic, dizziness, problems sleeping, cold or sweaty hands or feet, difficulty breathing, a racing heart, an inability to be calm, nausea, muscle tension, and tingling in the hands or feet. The most common anxiety disorders that can impact teens are briefly summarized below.

Panic disorder. People with panic disorder get surges of intense fear that seem to hit them out of the blue. These alarming episodes make them feel frozen. When teens with panic disorder describe the episode afterward, they say things like: "It's really scary. My chest was pounding, and I felt like I couldn't breathe." Or "I just froze up." Some even say it felt like they were "going crazy." Usually the panic is triggered by being in a certain type of situation. For example, one of my clients felt very self-conscious whenever he would break out in a sweat, so much so that he spiraled into panic.

Social anxiety disorder. People with social anxiety disorder experience huge worries and feel super self-conscious about everyday social situations. For example, they feel as though everyone is looking at them and negatively judging them, even though they know deep down this may not be true. Teens with social anxiety disorder usually worry about being seen as a loser or an outcast. Or they are constantly on edge about doing something that causes them embarrassment or shame.

Specific phobias. These are intense fears of specific things or situations—fears that are usually way out of proportion to those things or situations. Phobias lead people to avoid ordinary situations such as sharing the street with dogs (if they have a phobia of dogs) or going to the top floor of a building (if they have a phobia of heights).

Generalized anxiety disorder. People with generalized anxiety feel stressed out almost constantly. They describe feeling as if their anxiety switch is stuck in the "on position"—even when there's nothing around to trigger it. Their worries are over the top and cause a lot of tension.

If you think you may have an anxiety disorder, or if your worries are accompanied by depression or by intense, difficult-to-manage feelings, please see a qualified mental health professional (the appendix has a helpful guide for getting professional support).

So What Can You Do About Worry?

Knowing that worry isn't helpful and has negative consequences, how can you keep your everyday worries from spinning out of control and causing you big-time problems later on? There are many roads that appear to lead out of worry wasteland, but some of them will have you going in circles. If you've tried any of the following ways of avoiding worry, you probably know what I'm talking about.

Unhealthy Ways of Managing Worries

Here are some examples of ways that teens may manage their worries that don't turn out so well. If you have tried some of these, don't feel bad—we're all human.

HANGING OUT ON AVOIDANCE AVENUE

As a teen, when you feel upset, you probably just want to get rid of that feeling. Most teens say they just want to feel normal and that it is a bad thing to feel scared, angry, or sad. You may similarly feel that being okay and in control of your life means not feeling strong negative emotions. It is natural to want to avoid situations that bother you, but actually avoiding them doesn't help you succeed in life. If you keep avoiding starting that school project because you worry it won't be good enough, then you won't get a good grade or you may fail it. Worse, if avoidance becomes a pattern, it can eventually lead to skipping school after convincing yourself that you don't feel well. Similarly, if you avoid starting a conversation with that guy or girl you like because it makes you uncomfortable, then you won't get to know him or her.

ACTING OUT WITH ANGER

Sometimes our worries can get mixed up with other emotions. One emotion that very commonly gets jumbled up with worrying is anger. In my counseling practice, many moms and dads of teens seem to catch the brunt of their kids' frustration and anger. This can really leave them feeling hurt. And, as you probably know, being on the "Bottle It Up and Explode Later

Plan" will not lessen your worries or solve your problems. If you let the primitive part of your brain get overly activated with racing thoughts until you finally "flip your lid," you'll be unable to use the frontal part of your brain. And that's the part that does the reasoning and problem-solving, which are more helpful than the "fight, flight, or freeze" response for most challenges that come your way.

USING DRUGS OR ALCOHOL, SELF-HARM/ RECKLESS BEHAVIORS

Sadly, many teens (and adults) turn to unhealthy ways to manage worries. Many of my teen clients say they have tried drinking alcohol or smoking marijuana and using other drugs. Some teens value these drugs, yet most of them seem to have a hard time seeing that stress and worries are usually connected with drug use. Engaging in self-harming behaviors such as cutting is another unhealthy way of escaping your worries.

One client of mine who sometimes cut herself also described to me how she was acting out by engaging in promiscuous sex. She said that her worries about being "ugly" led her to impulsively seek validation through sexual encounters that ultimately left her feeling empty and ashamed.

EXCESSIVE SCREEN TIME

Using screen time as an escape from worries may not seem like a significant concern to some teens. Yet, the allure of social media, television shows, and video games can really become a problem when these digital distractions keep you from meeting demands and facing pressures in your life. For most teens, simply acknowledging how captivating screen time can be is an important step in setting and sticking to reasonable time limits.

Just Stop Worrying

Has anyone ever said to you something like, "You just need to stop worrying!"? If so, did it really help? Have you ever demanded of yourself that you stop worrying? I doubt that worked for you either.

This notion of "thought stopping" backfires because it forces you to pay extra attention to the very thoughts you want to avoid. You always have to be watching for them, which makes these unpleasant thoughts seem even more important. (There's a great exercise that proves it in chapter 4.)

Start Caring

As mentioned, worrying may feel like a good way to stay safe or to remember important things. Fortunately, I have found that most teens can learn to hold on to their need for security and still let go of worrying. They do this by shifting to a healthier way of thinking by seeing value in *caring* about their concerns as opposed to worrying about them.

Caring about your concerns is a far more helpful and productive use of your time than worrying about them. When you care about your needs, your goals, certain situations, or certain people, you're hopeful that things will go well. Caring keeps you from wasting energy by worrying. It helps you focus on doing what's important to you rather than avoiding what makes you uncomfortable. It helps you stay healthy and is good for your relationships with your family members and friends.

This powerful and very helpful shift from worrying to caring is really important and will be discussed in upcoming chapters. Teens tell me they feel relieved when they realize that they are not giving up their concerns by giving up their urge to worry. Once you unshackle yourself from the *urge* to worry, you'll be able to cope with your worries in a calmer way.

Teens in Their Own Words

"I'm worried about lots of stuff right now. It's my sophomore year, and—yeah, I know still have time—but honestly I'm freaking out about getting into a good college. I keep thinking about getting good grades and doing well in sports because I want to get a scholarship. Outside of school, I worry about guys thinking I'm cool and liking me and just being popular enough. And then there is all the drama with my friends who get all uptight. I guess I get a false sense of security by worrying and thinking it helps make things turn out better. This is so ridiculous though, because I know this is so not true. Being filled with worries actually just makes me moody and not fun for everyone else to be around me. I've learned that I can care about these concerns without feeling that I have to worry about them. What a relief!" ——Jody, age seventeen

Being open to your feelings, whether they're positive or negative, will help you understand and manage them. Staying aware of your worries and other negative feelings and mindfully acknowledging them will help you manage them and make better choices. It may seem counterintuitive, but once you have practiced really noticing your feelings, paying attention to them and focusing on them in ways you'll learn in this book, it will become easier to let those feelings go. Don't believe that you *can* let go? Take some time to think about the things you've likely already let go of. They may include:

- Fear of the dark

- Fear of going to class

- Fear of meeting new people

- Fear of being home alone

- Fear of wild animals or supernatural creatures

try this! Seeing You Can Let Go

Make a list of things that other people your age worry about that you yourself don't fret over. Maybe that list includes heights, bees, snakes, thunderstorms, speaking up in class, meeting new people, playing sports, or singing in public. Now make a list of the things you *have* worried about in the past but do not worry about any longer.

Afterward, look over your lists. Can you see how you have altogether avoided or gotten out of worry wasteland in the past? Do you feel encouraged by looking at how you have overcome past worries?

In this chapter, you learned that dwelling on the past or the future (teen minds tend to especially dwell on future concerns) can put you in the express lane to worry wasteland. You also learned how the primitive part of your brain—your "reacting brain"—is the place where worries develop. Your "thinking brain," not your "reacting brain," is what will help you successfully face the challenges of being a teen today. We also discussed why the things you may have tried or may currently be doing to manage your worries can be unhealthy or make your worries worse.

The next chapter will introduce you to mindfulness, which is all about living in the present. Learning about mindfulness and doing the exercises in this book will teach you to notice your worries in a new way, a way that doesn't make you stressed out and miserable. You'll practice not reacting to your worries so much. Eventually you'll have fewer worries in the first place. By the end of this book, you'll know surefire techniques to help you be happier, be more focused, and feel more confident when facing challenges.

chapter 2

the magic of mindfulness

The present moment is filled with joy and happiness. If you are attentive, you will see it.

—Thich Nhat Hanh

In chapter 1, we discussed how when you worry, you waste mental energy by focusing your thoughts on the past or future. Continuing to worry—to dwell on the fear of what bad things might happen—just makes your worries escalate; trying to ignore your worries is just wishful thinking and does not make them go away either. It is better to be mindful—to observe your worries without reacting to them and then let them go.

"What ifs" can get teens worried big-time. Let's say someone you know is planning a party, but you don't receive an invitation on social media. *What if my Instagram friends notice that I was not invited to that party?* Your mind starts to spin with thoughts of all the negative things your friends might think and say about you. This leads to more "What ifs" buzzing all around in your head. *What if my friends think I'm not cool anymore? What if...?*

Some teens struggle in silence, keeping these overwhelming "What ifs" to themselves. Others seek reassurance from friends and family members. Here is an exercise to help you begin to manage those "What ifs" by using mindfulness. Mindfulness is about focusing your awareness on the present moment, while acknowledging feelings, thoughts, and sensations without judgment.

try this! Noticing "What Ifs" Without Judging or Reacting to Them

Find a quiet space, sit in a relaxed position, and, if you want to, close your eyes. Teens generally tell me they prefer to close their eyes when doing mindfulness exercises by themselves, but if you are more comfortable at any time with your eyes open, that's fine too.

When you're settled and ready, begin to again notice your "What ifs" as you did in the last chapter. Don't try to ignore, fight, or control them. Instead, simply observe them from an outsider's perspective, without reacting or judging. Resist the temptation to answer the questions, to try to know the unknowable. Just let each "What if" hang there for a while in your mind.

Realize that those "What ifs" are just thoughts like any other random thoughts. (For example, if you're looking around your living room and kitchen, your thoughts might go like this: *The carpet is tan, but I wonder how this room would look if it was blue. The dishes are dirty. What if I don't finish the dishes before Dad gets home?* Yes, Dad would likely appreciate you getting those dishes done. Reacting differently in general, though, to those "What if" thoughts is a super-important way to not get so worked up about your worries.) Does that observation help you feel any differently—less worried than usual—when you have those "What if" thoughts?

30

As a variation of this exercise, look around at your current surroundings and notice as many things as you can. Notice the difference between "what if" and seeing "what is." Reflecting on "what is" in your surroundings takes you away from worrying about "what if." You might notice, for example, some cool details you usually passed over about a picture in your room or in the hallway. Maybe you're noticing the mesmerizing way the light reflects from a lamp or from your window; the gentle, soothing sound of a clock ticking; or other household sounds such as a washing machine or a television in another room.

Mindfulness gives you a new way to get out of worry wasteland and get back into your life. It is a well-established, reliable way to feel calmer. In fact, it has been used for thousands of years to promote emotional well-being. In recent years, scientific studies have repeatedly validated its positive effects on emotional, physical, and spiritual health.

All mindfulness techniques are a form of meditation. Meditation simply means focusing your awareness. Remember the hand model of your brain, from chapter 1? Mindfulness helps you use your higher brain (the thinking part) to calm down the swelling emotions of your lower brain (the reacting part). Realizing that your worries are just thoughts helps you see where they are coming from and is the first step to letting them go.

Name Your Worry to Tame Your Worry

Your "primitive brain" pushes worries on you. When you take time to be mindful, you are taming your primitive brain. There's an expression in mindfulness: "Name it to tame it." The act of naming your worries engages your "thinking brain," which tames and calms down your "reacting brain."

Carly's Story

Carly, age thirteen, had anger issues, and life as a seventh-grader was much harder than she had expected. She complained to me about "mega girl drama" and that "ridiculous amounts of homework" were stressing her out to the max. When I showed her the hand model of the brain in one of our early counseling sessions, she told me she could almost imagine her amygdala exploding on the spot!

Carly learned to tame her brain by mindfully learning to say: "Okay, this is what I am thinking and feeling right now. I don't have to do anything about my thoughts and feelings. I can just sit with them before I react or make any choice." Naming it to tame it also helped Carly notice that underlying her anger were worries of being rejected by her peers and not doing well in a particular class at school.

Mindfulness will help you appreciate joys and notice challenges in life without overreacting to them. It will create positive energy in your life and attract people to you. By practicing mindfulness, you will feel emotionally lighter and less stressed out. Eventually, others will likely pick up on your brighter, more relaxed moods. They may then want to spend more time with you because it makes them feel happier themselves.

Mindfulness is easy to learn, once you understand what it really is. Some people have misunderstandings about mindfulness. When they think of mindfulness, they associate it with constantly enlightened, blissfully happy Buddhist monks without a worry in the world, as portrayed in movies (unrealistic). Maybe some people even think mindfulness involves holding crystals containing special powers to escape the feelings of everyday stress. Before we go further, let's take a look at what mindful-ness is and what it is not.

Mindfulness Is...	Mindfulness Is Not...
noticing your thoughts and sensations.	making your mind a "blank slate" or stopping all thoughts.
having awareness of your breath, body, and mind.	a mysterious technique that takes years to learn.
noticing what is going on in the moment.	achieved only by meditating for hours at a time.
re-centering yourself to cope and gain hope.	sitting and drowning in worries or misery.
reacting to worries in a different way.	learning to never worry again.

Okay, now that you have a sense of what mindfulness really is, let's get into more detail about how it will help you manage your worries.

Getting Mindful to Feel Calmer and Happier

Being human involves facing uncertainties and stressful situ-ations, and, lo and behold, that means having things to worry about. The good news is that you don't have to stop yourself from getting worries in order to feel less stressed out and happier.

You simply have to learn to notice your thoughts, feelings, and physical sensations in the present moment without judgment. This will help you stop dwelling in all the strong emotions that can cloud your mind. Mindfulness strategies are helpful not only when you're feeling worried but also when you're moody, when you're angry, or when you just need to relax. If you feel as though right now your worries—or your moods—run your life, then changing how you react to your thoughts and emotions will get you back in control!

Wait—So Mindfulness Will Not Stop My Worries?

This book will not stop worries from creeping or jumping into your mind. But keep reading! Rather than completely remove worries, practicing mindfulness changes your relationship with your worries. It's about (1) noticing when your mind wanders to anxious thoughts and (2) gently bringing it back to a calmer state by focusing on what you're actually doing. Some of the simplest things we humans do are breathe, eat, and walk, so these are great activities to focus on when you first learn how to be mindful—or, rather, when you first learn how to be mindful on purpose. Because, believe it or not, you have already experienced many mindful moments.

You Already Know How to Be Mindful

You already have sampled the rich, powerful benefits of mindfulness. Think about those moments of joy in your life when you really noticed what was around you. At those times, you were being mindful by being aware of what was going on in the present moment.

Here are some examples. Have you ever:

Watched a beautiful, peaceful sunset and felt that it was a magical experience?

Walked outside and loved the feeling of the gentle breeze or the warm sun on your skin?

Petted a dog or a cat and been fully absorbed in the exchange of affection?

Listened to music and felt emotionally and spiritually moved, as though you were part of the music?

Hung out with friends and felt as though the time just melted away?

Cleaned your room and felt so "in the groove" while tidying and organizing that you were amazed at how much you got done?

Done just one thing at a time and felt super-focused?

If you have done any of these things—and I bet you have—you really do know what mindfulness is.

There are two ways to practice mindfulness. *Informal practice* involves having a moment-to-moment awareness of things like really feeling the gentle, warm breeze when you're walking outside. It's a way to be mindful as you go about your usual activities.

You don't have to watch a beautiful sunset or listen to wonderful music to informally practice mindfulness. In fact, being mindful while doing run-of-the-mill, "boring" daily activities can help you appreciate the best parts of these experiences.

For example, you can be mindful while brushing your teeth. Instead of thinking about something else as you brush, really try to focus on the refreshing feeling of having a cleaner mouth. I bet you'll be pleasantly surprised. Here are some other ways to informally practice mindfulness:

Take a shower, focusing on the warmth and comforting flow of the cleansing water.

Text a friend, focusing on how cool this form of instant communication is.

Play an instrument, focusing on the magic of creating musical sound.

Draw a picture, focusing on watching your own creative energy in action as you bring an image to life.

Exercise, focusing on really feeling your body and mind go through the motions.

Doing any everyday activity with a more focused awareness may bring you a little more joy or lighten your spirit.

The exercises in this book will not only strengthen your informal practice of mindfulness but also teach you how to do it a second way, as a formal practice. A formal practice involves actually setting aside time to be mindful—finding a quiet space where you can sit in a relaxed position and close your eyes if you want to. Mindfulness is called a "practice" for a reason—the more you do it, the better you'll get at it. Don't be intimidated or get discouraged when practicing seems hard. Don't pressure yourself to be perfect using mindfulness and have zero worries. The only perfect people are in the cemetery, and that is not where you want to be!

Why Does Mindfulness Help Manage Worries? A Closer Look

When you have mindful moments, you are not likely tuned in to your worries. A mindful moment with your friends may involve feeling really captivated by what your friends are saying. A mindful moment when you're walking outside may involve gazing in wonderment at the sparkling stars and pondering what lies beyond. When you start heading home on the school bus after a long day of hard classes and you look back at your school, maybe you feel a fantastic sense of freedom. Maybe you're mindful of that similar feeling of letting go after getting off work at your awful part-time job, and driving away from home in your car, or catching a ride with a friend. When you're focused on the good things in life, your worries seem to fade.

In the same way that you can't be hot when you are cold, or go fast when you are going slow, it's really not possible to be worried when you are mindfully relaxed. No longer will you honestly be able to say, "I can't stop worrying." How cool is that? Compared to worrying, mindfulness takes you to a better place.

Worrying Drives You to Be...	Mindfulness Gently Guides You to Be...
caught up in your own thoughts.	tuned in to the world around you with awareness.
negative, with a closed attitude.	curious and open in your attitude.
inflexible with your attention, narrowly focused.	flexible with your attention; broadly aware.
cynical and non-trusting.	positive and connected to others and new things.

Wouldn't it be great to learn how to get those mindful feelings and sensations whenever you want to have them? Look no further than your willingness and imagination. These are your prized tools that will get you out of worry wasteland. Any time you need a mental reboot, you can use them to connect to the present moment. If you make yourself fully aware of the present—not obsessing over the past or fretting about the future—you'll find it easier to cope or to get a boost of hope.

The Power of the Present Moment

During the writing of this book, I had some worries about whether my words would help you. When experiencing these worries, I paused to take a few deep, mindful breaths (as you will soon learn to do). I reminded myself that my worries were just thoughts and that I could let them just be there. Instead of worrying about whether you will like and value this book, I replayed in my mind a lesson that my client Sandy taught me. Check out how Sandy used mindfulness to manage her worries about making a presentation for one of her classes.

Sandy's Story

Sandy, a high-school freshman, was really worried because she had to give a presentation in class. When she took a time-out to mindfully reflect on her thoughts and jitters about the presentation, she started to calm down. And as she grew calmer, she realized that she owned her worried thoughts— they did not own her. This helped her feel less stressed and even got her pumped up to do the presentation, though she still had some worries.

She ended up receiving an A on the presentation. More importantly, though, during her presentation, Sandy had been able to mindfully shift from drowning in worries to focusing on caring about what she wanted to share with the class. "I just mindfully stayed in the unpleasantness of my scary thoughts without judging myself. This helped me shift from thinking it had to be perfect to actually becoming excited to do the presentation."

Sandy learned, as you will too, that mindfulness helps you have less intense and fewer thoughts about the past or future. That is great news, because the less powerful your worries and the fewer worries you have, the easier it will be to handle them. We will discuss mindfulness strategies for school work in greater detail in chapter 6.

Now that you have a general sense of what mindfulness is and some ways to bring it into your life, let's break it down.

Three Parts of Mindfulness

Mindfulness is described in different ways by many writers and researchers. In her books and presentations, Shauna Shapiro, a noted mindfulness expert, says that mindfulness consists of three main components: intention, attention, and attitude.

Intention

Mindfulness is about gently intending to be aware. This means noticing your moment-by-moment experiences in an open and nonjudgmental way. It's about having awareness of this present moment—this one right now—compared to worrying, which (as mentioned) is being caught up in thoughts about the past or future. What does having an intention to be mindful look and feel like?

Well, teens with mindful intention:

- notice how they think and feel without judgment;

- observe their bodies, breath, and the world around them;

- notice their vulnerabilities; and

- see their strengths.

Attention

Mindfulness involves having flexible attention. This means focusing on different parts of what you are experiencing. Mindful attention is about willingly noticing everything in your life. This can help with how you choose to respond to your worries and the situations you encounter in life.

Attention, in a mindful sense, is not about comparing or judging what you experience. Instead, it is simply about noticing what is taking place right now. The opposite of mindfulness is mindlessness, being on automatic pilot. Have you ever walked into the wrong class? Embarrassing, right? We've all been there. I'll never forget the humiliating day I stepped in fresh cement on a sidewalk even though there were red flags clearly marking where to walk. Talk about having a mindless experience instead of a mindful one!

Teens with mindful attention:

- sit with thoughts and feelings and observe them before deciding what they mean;

- encourage themselves to take pleasure in what they are doing;

- value text messages and also value smiles in real-life, person-to-person encounters; and

- see worries as clouds passing by instead of as endless storms.

Attitude

When you are mindful, you have an open and curious attitude. Even if you currently are in a rough place, such as suddenly feeling as though your best friend is being distant toward you, you are open to and curious about that feeling instead of running from it or fighting it. It's almost as though you're doing and experiencing things in your life for the very first time. A way to think like this is to imagine you're an alien or a robot learning what it's like to be human. This attitude of curiosity is what many mindfulness writers call "beginner's mind."

People who practice mindfulness bring this attitude of curiosity with them throughout the day. So when you take a shower mindfully, you might imagine it's your first time feeling the water, smelling the soap, or watching the steam as it shifts and changes before your eyes.

Teens with a mindful attitude:

- strive to accept themselves and others without judgment;

- feel compassion (a deep sense of caring and concern) for themselves and others;

- see their world with beginner's mind by feeling a sense of curiosity about the things and people around them and by noticing sensations, thoughts, and feelings going on within themselves; and

- are authentic by freely expressing themselves while respecting others' feelings.

Turning to NOW

The acronym NOW can help you bring in intention, attention, and attitude for practicing mindfulness. NOW stands for:

(N) Noticing what is around you

(O) Opening up your curiosity

(W) Willingly letting go of unhelpful, distracting thoughts and feelings

Tony, a fifteen-year-old client of mine, was worried that he could not come up with the "right things" to say when he was with his friends. He used NOW for mindfulness when coping with those worries.

(N): Tony noticed what he valued about being with his friends, how he felt when he was with them, and that not everything they said was perfect.

(O): He opened up his curiosity to listen to and learn about his friends rather than try to impress them.

(W): He willingly let go of thinking how "well" he was doing when talking with his friends.

The Benefits of Mindfully Letting Go of Your Worries

Mindfulness is a helpful and healthy way to stop your brain from tricking you into needlessly worrying. Remember Wes, from chapter 1, whose "What ifs" sent him on the express train to worry wasteland? I'm happy to share with you that being mindful enabled him to calm down. It allowed him to roll with, and even question, his "What if" thoughts. This gave him big-time relief from worrying about things that had not even yet occurred. (His worries were about school, so I'll tell you how he did it in chapter 6.)

Want to hear from teens who, after learning mindfulness, found themselves worrying less and feeling happier?

Teens in Their Own Words

"I was way too worried about stuff that probably would never happen, and mindfulness helped to calm me down."
—Celeste, age fourteen

"Mindfulness gave me strength to deal with really hard things going on in my life." —Trey, age fifteen

"I was a lot moodier before I started practicing mindfulness. Now I feel more patient and much happier."
—Evette, age fifteen

"My life was always about what I did in the past and what I was going to do in the future. By trying mindfulness, I'm less in my head and more in my life right now."
—Cameron, age seventeen

Mindfulness is not a miracle cure to stop your worries, but it will help keep them from controlling you. Over time, with practice, you can turn down the frequency and volume of those worry thoughts, and your brain will calm down. This will improve your ability to think clearly and realistically. Teens have said that mindfulness helps them:

feel calmer and less worried;

be happier and have a more positive attitude;

feel less angry and less likely to lash out;

have less test anxiety, pay better attention, and do better in school; and see friends and family members as wanting to hang out with them because they're less focused on themselves.

When you practice mindfulness (and it really is an ongoing practice versus something you master), your life will feel way calmer.

The next chapter will introduce you to some "formal" practices of mindfulness. Don't let the word "formal" scare you away. "Formal" mindfulness practice just means taking time out of your day to be mindful. These upcoming exercises will open up and re-center your mind to live in the moment—much freer of worries than you have ever been before!

In the chapters that follow, you will learn to free yourself from the worries that dominate your thoughts and get in your way. You'll do activities like breathing with awareness, paying attention to your body in a special way, focusing on your five senses to keep you mentally centered, and observing your wandering thoughts. The more you reflect on how these practices calm you down and help you feel better, the more likely you'll want to do them again.

chapter 3

the beginner's mindfulness tool kit

You learned about why you worry in chapter 1. In chapter 2 you found out what mindfulness is and what it is not. As an introduction to practicing mindfulness in chapter 2, you noticed your "What ifs" in a mindful way and learned about the power of NOW to help you break free from the shackles and chains of useless worries. The exercises in this chapter will help you see the many roads that can lead you out of worry wasteland. Getting moving on a mindful path can help you pursue whatever your worries are holding you back from, such as talking to that hot guy or girl in your gym class, trying out for a new sport, or seeking a part in the school play. How cool is that?

First, Some Brief Words of Encouragement

The magic of mindfulness comes from you practicing. As you move through this chapter, keep in mind that you are allowed to like some exercises more than others. Some of the exercises you may not like at all. That said, you owe it to yourself to have a "Keep serving me up" mentality. What I mean by this is it's not fair to decide mindfulness exercises won't work even before you try them, and it's not in your best interest to do them only halfheartedly.

Just like practicing an instrument, training for a sport, or learning a new language, being mindful is a practice too. Please be open-minded and patient. The exercises in this book are the ones teens I know have found most appealing and helpful. The time you spend "staying in" and repeating the exercises throughout this book is up to you. Do what feels comfortable, and gently encourage yourself to do a little more if you're willing.

Your Breath Is an Anchor for Mindfulness

Breathing mindfully is a very effective way to manage your worried mind, which is why it's part of many exercises throughout this book. Noticing your breathing is a very centering, reliable way to focus on what is going on in the present moment, and this is why it is considered as an anchor for mindfulness. Since you have to breathe all the time anyway, why not take time to breathe mindfully every day? Making mindful breathing part of your daily routine will go a long way toward helping you feel less stressed out. Let's briefly highlight why mindful breathing, when done correctly, will be a really helpful part of managing your worries.

By focusing on your breath, you bring your awareness to the present moment—the cornerstone of mindfulness. Being in the present moment shifts your awareness away from the worries in your head and quiets your mind. One way to breathe mindfully is to simply notice your breath as it is: notice whether it's fast or slow, shallow or deep, without judgment. You may certainly do all the exercises in this book in that manner.

However, I encourage you to, while keeping an attitude of nonjudgment, gently extend your in-breaths deeper into your belly. This is because deep, mindful "belly breathing" increases the supply of oxygen to your brain, helps you think more clearly, and signals your body to relax.

The way your deep, mindful breath actually relaxes your body is really cool. Your breath is part of a feedback loop with your nervous system. When you're on edge—like when you're agitated, excited, or scared—you breathe quickly and shallowly. This type of breathing, called chest breathing, helps your body prepare for action. Your heart rate and blood pressure increase, and you feel more alert to potential dangers. This cause-and-effect relationship works in the other direction too: when you breathe quickly and shallowly, you feel more on edge. Try it and see. It's certainly hard to relax while breathing this way, isn't it?

Now let's contrast chest breathing with belly breathing. When your breath flows into the lower part of your lungs (did you know your lungs extend all the way down below your lowest ribs?), and you expand your belly like a balloon (referred to as belly breathing), it stimulates the nerve called your vagus nerve. The vagus nerve is part of a group of nerves that help shift you out of stress mode. By activating your vagus nerve beginning with your first deep belly breath, your heart rate slows, your blood pressure drops, and you feel more relaxed.

Think of a car racing down the highway at 120 miles an hour. That's you in stress mode, and your vagus nerve is the brake. When you are stressed, it's as if you're pushing the gas pedal to the floor. Slow, deep, mindful breaths can become your trusty brake pedal.

To learn mindful breathing with deeper breaths, as described in the next exercise, place one hand on your chest and one on your belly (below your rib cage and above your belly button). Teens tell me that doing this really helps them literally feel their breaths. As you gently breathe in, focus on drawing your breath in through your nostrils, noticing how it feels as it passes through your trachea and down into your belly. You will notice that, with each breath, the hand on your chest moves only a little, while the hand on your belly more noticeably rises with each in-breath and sinks down with each out-breath. This is the opposite breathing pattern of rapid, chest breathing, which is how we tend to breathe when we're worried.

Keep in mind the placement of your hands on your chest and belly as you do the following exercise. (An audio version is available at http://www.newharbinger.com/39812.)

try this! Being Mindful by Noticing Your Breath

Day and night, in good times and bad, whether you're at home, at school, or at work, your breath is always there for you, to keep you alive and nourish your body and your mind. Noticing your breath is a great way to start practicing mindfulness.

To prepare for this exercise and most of the ones that follow in this book, unless the directions suggest otherwise, simply find a quiet place and sit comfortably. Once you're settled, if it feels right to you, let your eyes gently close. Or you can gaze softly at a spot a few feet in front of you, looking at nothing in particular.

1. Focus your attention on your breath.

2. Place one hand on your chest and one on your belly,

3. As you breathe in, say to yourself, *I'm breathing in.*

4. Pay attention to the sensations of your breath passing into your body.

5. As you breathe out, say to yourself, *I'm breathing out.*

6. Observe the sensations in your body related to your out-breath.

7. Notice whether your attention is on your breath or whether it has wandered to thoughts about other things.

8. Continue to gently maintain your awareness on or return your awareness to your breath.

9. Repeat steps 1 through 8 four times.

Afterward, reflect on what was it like to pay attention to your breath and the sensations of it passing through your body. What was it like to come back to the present moment when you noticed your attention had wandered? Did you notice anything interesting or surprising? Can you see how mindful breathing offers you a soothing way to re-center yourself and move out of worry wasteland?

Check out what other teens have said about mindful, deep breathing.

Teens in Their Own Words

"Mindful breathing was easy for me to learn, and it has seriously helped keep me out of trouble by calming me down. I also don't say upsetting things that I regret as much."
—Jayden, age fourteen

"Just knowing that a couple of mindful breaths are always there to center me if I need them has really helped me feel less uptight and worried when I am walking through the crowded hallways at school." —Olivia, age sixteen

Making mindful breathing a consistent practice can really help you feel calmer. Assuming you are just starting out with mindfulness, I recommend you begin by breathing mindfully for one minute each night before bed. Teens share with me that doing mindful breathing before going to bed helps them sleep better. Or take some mindful breaths in the morning before going to school, to help set the tone for a more relaxed day. As stresses and upsetting thoughts pop up, you can take some mindful breaths to re-center yourself any time of day, wherever you may be.

If you want to breathe mindfully for two minutes, five minutes, or even longer, that's great. Just remember that to get the most benefit from mindfulness exercises, being consistent and practicing daily (or at least a few times per week) is better than practicing infrequently but for longer. Also, starting out trying to be a "mindfulness machine" by doing mindfulness exercises for an hour every day may lead to you burn out and bail on mindfulness. To keep your practice sustainable, start with briefer periods, such as one to two minutes, and gradually build up to more time if you want to do so. The most important thing is that you strive to practice mindfulness on a regular basis.

The opportunities to use your breath to feel less weighed down in the present moment are as vast as all those wandering thoughts in your head. Teens tell me that a bit of mindful breathing helps them let go of worries and troublesome thoughts like these:

- "What if they all ignore me at the dance?"

- "I'm so lost in this class, and I'm definitely going to fail the test on Friday."

- "My life feels unfair."

- "I so can't wait to be done listening to this teacher."

- "This dull classroom makes me feel trapped in negativity."

- "Those kids are going to make me feel like crap if they come up and talk to me."

When these kinds of thoughts and worries come up, take a few mindful breaths. As your body relaxes, so will your thoughts and fears. To increase the effectiveness of mindful breathing, if you have the opportunity, you can add a bit of visualization to help you calm down and have more trust in your ability to get through tough times.

try this! Branching Out with the Breath Exercise

Breathe in, imagining you are connected to the ground like the roots of a tree. With each out-breath, see yourself letting go of your worries. Visualize a tree bending with the wind, not breaking. Gently try to hold that image in your mind for about a minute. As you think of this strong yet flexible tree, accept whatever thoughts, sensations, or emotions blow your way. Let them pass you by like so many molecules of air, even your worries. Repeat this exercise one or two more times if you want to.

Afterward, think about how it felt to draw upon the strength and flexibility of the tree while doing your breathing. Did visualizing the tree give you a sense of strength or confidence? Were you able to feel more sensations in your breath or body as you identified yourself with the tree image?

Remember, You Are in a No-Judgment Zone

As mentioned, some exercises in this book may appeal more to you than others. Some days you may even want to say, "This mindfulness stuff is a waste of time." Feel free to just let these thoughts exist as they are. I have found, in my own mindfulness practice, that sometimes I just don't want to do it. I realized that these are just feelings and that they are okay.

However, on days that I do not practice mindfulness, I experience more stress as a result. By the same token, the more often I am mindful (even for brief periods of time), the less intensely and less often I am worried. I also feel calmer and happier when

I am being mindful. The teens I know who practice mindfulness tell me the same goes for them.

Still, I try not to pressure myself to be mindful, and I hope you won't either. Don't judge yourself if you feel resistant to practicing or decide to skip doing formal mindfulness at times. If you really don't feel like doing it that day, then don't. Mindfulness will always welcome you back without judgment, even if days, weeks, or months have gone by since you last used it. The teens I know smile a lot more when they lessen the pressure they put on themselves to do things like be mindful every day. Speaking of smiling, a smile is a universal way of communicating that things are going well and it has been shown to generate positivity in the person doing the smiling, as well as to spread good feelings. Try noticing how it feels to smile from the inside out in the following exercise. (An audio version is available at http://www.newharbinger.com/39812.)

try this! Sending Your Inner Smile to Your Outer World

When it comes to calming yourself, gently starting your smile from within can feel very soothing. In this exercise, you'll see what it feels like to mindfully smile first within yourself and then caringly send it to the world around you.

But first, let me reach out to you smile resisters. Maybe you feel as though you have too much to worry about right now to smile about anything. I really do get it if you normally hesitate or hold back on smiling. That said, and I am smiling as I write this, if you can gently encourage yourself to give this exercise a go, you may like it more than you think you will. If you're not pleasantly surprised, you don't have to do it again!

1. Take a few mindful breaths in and out.

2. Close your eyes and let a slight smile form on your lips. To help your smile along, reflect on those fun times with friends or think of some funny videos or movie scenes that lift your mood.

3. As you breathe in, send your smile along with your breath to soothe you throughout your body. Feel your centering, nourishing breath fill the back of your throat, moving down your windpipe, into your chest, and down into your abdomen.

4. As you breathe out, visualize your smile moving outside of you. Imagine your smile floating through the air and touching everyone and everything you see.

5. Repeat this a few times.

Afterward, reflect on the experience. What was it like to smile from the inside out? How might smiling from the inside out help free you from worries? What can smiling from the inside teach you about yourself? How might beginning your smile from the inside help you connect to the world around you and lessen your frustrations with friends, family members, teachers, and coworkers?

Now that you've tried a new way of smiling, it's time to explore a new way of eating. Yes, eating can be a great way of mindfully centering yourself. Because, like breathing, eating is something we all do. And, hopefully, you do it on a regular basis (!), so it's a good way to build a regular practice of mindfulness.

Getting into Eating Awareness

Have you ever heard someone ask a person who seems troubled, "What's eating *you*?" This figure of speech describes how our worries can really consume our attention and distract us from what's going on in the present moment. If you can literally learn to eat mindfully, this is a great way to get past being stuck in worries and reorient yourself to being in the present.

One way to think about mindfulness is to consider how people sometimes eat on autopilot, without paying attention to their food. Think about how often you yourself eat while doing something else. Some teens do three or four things at a time while eating! Mobile devices have certainly made this kind of multitasking very common. Have you ever noticed families sitting at a restaurant with parents and kids absorbed in their phones? These family members are not really focused on truly enjoying their meal, or for that matter even each other!

Perhaps you feel as if eating is a chore, something you need to do, like filling your car up with gas. In today's hectic world— especially if you like to stay busy or have made it a habit to stay busy, as a way of pushing worries out of your mind—you may feel as though eating while *not* doing something else is wasting time. Or, maybe you believe that eating, in and of itself, or while you're doing something else, like when trying to study or even when relaxing and watching a movie, is a "calm down reward" that you feel you deserve or just plain want to have. But you will likely value the experience of slowing down. Eating is an important activity, and you can strive to enjoy the experience of eating, not just the sensation of feeling full afterward. Noticing how you experience your food is a great way to gain awareness, which is key to becoming more mindful. It may even help you not overeat when you're stressed.

One cool mindfulness exercise was developed by a well-known mindfulness researcher and practitioner named Jon Kabat-Zinn. It involves mindfully eating a raisin. I love this exercise, because it helps you slow down and pay attention to what is really going on when you lift a bite of food to your mouth. It's like eating with all your senses, not just your sense of taste. Try this activity as described below to experience eating in perhaps a different way than you ever have before. (An audio version is available at http://www.newharbinger.com/39812.)

try this! Eating Mindfully

For this activity, you will need a raisin or any food you would like to substitute, such as another piece of fruit, a piece of popcorn, a piece of gum, a chunk of chocolate, or a small piece of bread. (We'll just refer to it as "the raisin.")

1. Sit comfortably in a chair.

2. Place the raisin in the palm of your hand.

3. Examine the raisin as if you had never seen it before (with beginner's mind, as discussed in chapter 2).

4. Imagine what the raisin must have looked like when it was a grape growing on a vine. Imagine its plumpness, growing under the sun, surrounded by nature.

5. As you look at the raisin, be conscious of every aspect of what you see: the shape, texture, color, size. Hold the raisin up to the light. Does the raisin look hard or soft, dry or moist?

6. Bring and hold the raisin to your nose. Notice its aroma. Are you anticipating eating the raisin? Is it difficult to resist the temptation to pop it in your mouth?

7. How does the raisin feel in your hand? Gently squeeze the raisin and experience it with your sense of touch.

8. Place the raisin in your mouth. Become aware of how it feels on your tongue.

9. Bite slowly into the raisin. Feel its softness and squishiness (or its hardness and crunchiness).

10. Chew three times and then stop.

11. Notice the flavor of the raisin. What is the texture?

12. Finish chewing, and swallow the raisin. What sensations do you notice as you swallow it?

13. Sit quietly, breathing, aware of what you are sensing as a result of just having swallowed the raisin. Notice how your body and mind are feeling now having completed this mindful eating exercise.

Can you see how being mindful at mealtimes can become an opportunity to reflect on a much broader and deeper experience? A simple piece of food, such as a raisin, is connected to nature. In a way, having grown from a seed, it holds within it all the elements of nature: the earth, wind, rain and sunshine. And if you eat a salad, a pasta, or other complex dish, you can imagine all the people from around the world who managed the ingredients and put them together. Experiencing your food in a new way, with mindful curiosity, allows you to get back in touch with feeling bigger things in life than your worries—all the wonders within and around you.

You can feel gratitude and recognize the interconnection of all things.

Try eating mindfully in different places—at home, in the school cafeteria, or in a restaurant. You can even do it in the car—but if you're the one behind the wheel, then please, only when parked! Following is a shorter mindfulness exercise involving your imagination and your senses of taste and smell.

try this! A Mindful Cup of Hot Chocolate

The hot (and cool) thing about this exercise is that you can practice breathing and using your senses without focusing on your breath or chewing on a piece of food. For teens I see who are more reluctant to try mindfulness, I tell them to put mindfulness aside and just think about hot chocolate. Happily, most teens, and I as well, love hot choc-olate. But if hot chocolate is not appealing to you, try using or imagin-ing hot apple cider, tea, or your favorite soup. This exercise is an easy, brief way to begin exploring mindfulness.

1. Quietly and slowly breathe in through your nose as you smell (or imagine smelling) a mug of hot chocolate.

2. Exhale by blowing through your mouth to cool the beverage off.

3. Repeat this four times.

Afterward, reflect on your experience of this hot-chocolate-breathing exercise. Could you taste the chocolate with your mind as you breathed in the aroma? Did it smell pleasurable? Could you feel yourself cooling the beverage down as you breathed out?

The previous exercise helped you mindfully tune in to your senses of taste and smell. Let's now look to another one of your senses to practice mindfulness: your sense of sight.

try this! Noticing with Camera Eyes

The reason we value cameras, including those on our phones, is they allow us to literally hold on to images. In this exercise, you will experience mindfulness by focusing on what is around you and holding onto that image with a heightened sense of awareness.

1. Take a few mindful breaths and relax, either sitting or standing.

2. Look around you for a minute or so and notice everything you can.

3. Close your eyes and visualize all you can remember of what you saw around you.

4. Open your eyes again, and compare what you see to what you remembered.

Afterward, reflect on the experience. How closely did the picture you took in your mind match up with was really there? Can you see how you were tuned into the moment, not likely focusing on your worries? Can you give yourself the gift of nonjudgment about how well you did?

We can also notice our sense of hearing to practice mindfulness. There are so many sounds that reach our ears, but we often shut them out. Think about the voice of your most boring teacher as just one example of this. Ugh! Check out this special way of noticing what you hear around you.

try this! Now Hear This

1. Take a few relaxing, mindful breaths.

2. Listen to the sounds around you for about a minute.

3. Pick one sound, and focus in on it. Notice everything you can about this sound and its qualities. Is it soft or loud? High-pitched or low-pitched? Intermittent or constant? Is it tinny or full-sounding? How does it vary as you listen to it?

4. If distracting thoughts pop up, gently bring your attention back to this sound. Keep listening for about a minute.

5. Shift your attention to another sound. (If there is no other audible sound, then imagine one, such as ocean waves or cars passing by, or use a video channel or mobile app to softly play a sound). Do your best, without judgment, to notice and tune into this second sound for about another minute, observing all its qualities, as you did with the first sound.

6. Go back to the first sound and keep your attention on it for about thirty seconds, then focus again on the second sound instead. After about thirty seconds, switch again. Do this a couple more times if you want to.

7. Try to hold both the first and second sounds in your mind *at the same time*. Keep it up for about fifteen to thirty seconds if you're comfortable doing so.

What was this mindful listening exercise like for you? Did your mindful attention make the sounds more or less pleasurable? Did you get frustrated when switching between sounds, or did you just accept the experience without judgment? Is mindfully noticing the sounds around you something you have taken for granted over the years?

As a concluding exercise for this chapter, try putting three of your senses together.

try this! Tuning into Mindfulness with Three Senses

Sit down on a couch or a chair, and take a few slow, mindful breaths. Ask yourself:

1. **What are three things that you can see?** For example, you can see the wall in front of you, a lamp, and a table. Do your best for about a minute or two, without pressuring yourself, to simply notice the colors, textures, shapes of what you see. Simply notice what you are seeing right now. Don't feel a need to notice any one thing more than another.

2. **What are three things that you can hear?** For example, you can hear the sounds of traffic, people's voices, and a clock ticking. Just experience these sounds without judgment for a minute or two.

3. **What are three things that your body is touching?** For example, you're sitting on the couch, holding this book, and resting on a pillow. Pay attention to the impression they create on your sense of touch.

As you can see, there are many interesting ways to be mindful even when doing the simplest things. Remember, formal exercises don't have to feel like work, though they take some effort on your part. If you can make it a point to do at least one of these exercises a day, or even a few times a week, and for just a few minutes, you will likely feel less worried and less stressed out. Keep in mind, the more often you practice mindfulness, the calmer and happier you will likely feel.

Teens in Their Own Words

"Mindfulness is taking a moment to legitimately give yourself a mental break and stop being so busy. It reduces all expectations." —Linda, age eighteen

In the next chapter, you will learn to use an accepting, flexible attitude to get past obstacles you may encounter on your mindful path out of worry wasteland.

chapter 4

getting back in control by letting go

Whatever you fight, you strengthen, and what you resist, persists.

—Eckhart Tolle

When you're being mindful, all kinds of thoughts can pop up. Some of those thoughts may be encouraging, and others may be discouraging. From time to time, you may have thoughts like these:

- *I was distracted. I'll never get it right.*

- *Why am I wasting my time doing this mindfulness stuff? I could be doing something about my worries right now instead of just focusing on my breath.*

- *I'm just no good at this. Maybe I don't have the right kind of brain.*

- *This is too hard. Ugh.*

- *I practiced mindfulness yesterday, and today I'm just as worried as ever. It must not be working.*

Many teens mistakenly think that being mindful means not having any distracting thoughts. They tell me things like, "I tried taking deep breaths, focusing on my senses, and visualizing things like you showed me, but mindfulness doesn't work because my head is filled with worries and other thoughts." Some adults also tell me that they tried practicing mindfulness but could not stick with it because they got too distracted.

Sadly, people who think they can't "get mindful enough" because of distracting thoughts may turn away from mindfulness before giving it a chance to help them. This sometimes happens when people mistakenly think that being mindful means trying to *change* or *control* their thoughts instead of just noticing and accepting them.

The quotation at the beginning of this chapter (from Eckhart Tolle, a famous spiritual teacher) is about how, when it comes to dealing with unpleasant or counterproductive thoughts—or any type of unwanted inner experience, such as a difficult emotion or annoying sensation—acceptance works better than resistance. This concept is related to mindfulness. Mindfulness isn't about controlling your thoughts; it's about having an accepting attitude toward all the different types of thoughts that arise in your mind—whether these are worry thoughts or any other kind of thoughts. Because, as strange as it may sound, if you stop trying to control your thoughts, you'll find that you don't get caught up in them as often.

Having an accepting attitude will support your practice of mindfulness. Acceptance of distracting thoughts, even including skeptical ones, can help you not give up when mindfulness seems too hard.

Acceptance of the struggles along on the path to mindfulness is, in and of itself, a huge part of what mindfulness is about.

So first let's look at how acceptance will help you break free of thoughts that might discourage you from practicing mindfulness. Then, we will discuss how acceptance more broadly will help free you of actual worry thoughts.

Practicing Mindfulness May Feel Challenging

I'm going to lend you my pink elephant to show you how accepting the distracting thoughts that move in and out of your awareness when you practice mindfulness is far more helpful than trying to snuff them out.

Ignoring Distracting Thoughts Is Like Trying Not to See a Pink Elephant

Sometimes teens tell me that trying to ignore distracting thoughts when practicing mindfulness is like trying to not notice a pink elephant standing in front of them. I respond to these frustrated teens by saying: "I understand! I often experience the same struggle!" When they hear that I, too, have trouble with distracting thoughts, they gain confidence in their own ability to be as mindful as anyone else. Mindfulness is not something that anyone does perfectly.

It is actually widely common to wonder, "Can I really be mindful and less worried with my distracted, racing mind?" The short answer is yes! Don't believe me? Then do the following exercise and answer the questions. (An audio version of this exercise is available at http://www.newharbinger.com/39812.)

try this! Seeing Beyond the Pink Elephant

Part 1. Close your eyes. Imagine, as vividly as you can, a bright pink elephant. Yes, bright pink! Visualize a very large pink elephant with a long, swaying pink trunk. Make the elephant start dancing.

Part 2. Okay, now close your eyes and try *not* to think about the pink elephant. Don't think about how big it is. Try not to think about its long, supple, swaying pink trunk. Make yourself think of anything else but the pink elephant. Keep doing this for a few minutes.

At the end of a few minutes, what are you thinking of? During those few minutes, how many times did the pink elephant cross your mind? Quite a few?

Part 3. Okay, now close your eyes again. Tell yourself that for this next part of the exercise, it doesn't matter whether you think about the pink elephant. Your goal now is to gently focus your attention on noticing your in-breath and out-breath, your bodily sensations, and the sights and sounds around you. Do this for a few minutes.

How many times did you think of the pink elephant this time? Zero? Maybe one or two?

Can you see how trying to force yourself to not think about the pink elephant was not helpful? Yet when you allowed yourself to accept that you may have thoughts about the pink elephant, you likely stopped pressuring yourself to exert control over your thoughts. This accepting attitude helped you mindfully notice your breath, your body, and the sights and sounds around you. The pink elephant likely no longer dominated your thoughts in the same way and began to fade into the background of your mind. The point is that telling yourself not to have certain kinds of thoughts, such as thoughts about a pink elephant, doesn't work. Acceptance, on the other hand, helps you move beyond those thoughts.

The pink elephant exercise helps teens realize that they can be mindful even when they have distracting thoughts. These include non-worried thoughts, such as *What will I eat for dinner?* and worried ones, such as *Did I just fail my math test?* Just as you learned with the pink elephant, being preoccupied with what sort of thoughts you don't want to have is bound to backfire. Accepting your distracting thoughts and gently refocusing yourself feels so much better, and is much easier, than trying to stop or control your thoughts. (By the way, if you find yourself never getting distracted again in your life after taking a few mindful breaths, then please contact me immediately and together we can write a very thin, new version of this book!)

Now let's discuss distracting beliefs that can get in the way of learning and practicing mindfulness. Many teens have learned how to overcome these obstacles by accepting rather than trying to control them, and you can too! Accepting your frustrations and doubts about practicing mindfulness makes it easier to use mindfulness for successfully managing your worries.

Getting Past Obstacles to Mindfulness

Following are six common obstacles teens struggle with as they try to learn and practice mindfulness. The common thread among them is that they are based on unhelpful, distorted beliefs about mindfulness itself. The key is to remember that these obstacles are unhelpful views—and like a pink elephant intruding on your thoughts, you can manage them if you notice and accept them in a different way. If you're up against these obstacles, you are essentially getting in your own way when it comes to being mindful.

1. BEING DISAPPOINTED THAT MINDFULNESS WON'T MAKE YOUR MIND A "BLANK SLATE"

As mentioned in chapter 2, mindfulness is not about making your mind a "blank slate" or focusing on just one thing. We challenged this misperception about mindfulness with the pink elephant exercise. This "blank slate" myth is crucial to address because it's a common reason why people say, "I can't be mindful." Or, "I can't meditate." As mentioned in chapter 2, rather than think too much about the terms "mindfulness" and "meditation" and your preconceptions of what they mean as a result of the way they're sometimes portrayed in popular culture, think of meditation as a form of being mindful. The bottom line is that attempting to control your mind by trying to make it blank is a huge misstep.

Teens in Their Own Words

"When I found myself thinking, 'I can't be mindful because I keep getting distracted by my thoughts,' I would gently remind myself: 'It is normal to have all kinds of thoughts going through my head. I don't have to try to empty out my thoughts. Gently redirecting my attention back to my breath, my body, or anything else I notice gives me even more opportunity to be mindful.'" —Laura, age seventeen

2. THINKING THAT MINDFULNESS BRINGS IMMEDIATE INNER PEACE

Even though the ability to be mindful is already within you, you need to give yourself time to let it really manifest.

Ben's Story

Ben, age sixteen, was frustrated in his attempts to be mindful. It turned out that he had a distorted, rigid idea of what mindfulness was about. In my counseling practice, he told me that he thought mindfulness was supposed to be a way of obtaining instant inner peace. He added, "I was curious about it and looked up some stuff online, and it seemed like a cool way to quickly chill out. I was hoping that mindfulness would totally make me quickly forget some crappy things that are bothering me. I tried being mindful, and it did not change anything, like nothing yet has really happened—I'm, like, seriously frustrated."

I told Ben that the more accepting and patient he was in his attitude toward mindfulness, the more he would feel the calming benefits of practicing mindfulness. Knowing that he had a good sense of humor, I shared a cartoon with him that I found online. It shows a frustrated woman in a yoga pose. The caption reads, "C'mon inner peace, I don't have all day." Ben posted this quote on his social media site and on his bedroom wall to remind him to be patient when practicing mindfulness.

After he accepted that he would not instantly become worry-free every time he practiced mindfulness, in just a few weeks he felt much calmer. His favorite mindfulness exercises were focusing on sounds around him (see chapter 3) and mindful walking (see chapter 5).

Ben was drawn to the concept of instant inner peace, and I can't say I blamed him. Instant inner peace sounds great. Who wouldn't love to take a few deep breaths and, presto, no longer have anything to worry about? But mindfulness takes time and practice, so it's important that you maintain realistic expectations. It's ironic but true that you'll feel more peaceful when you stop frantically searching for inner peace.

Teens in Their Own Words

"When practicing mindfulness, it helps me to just let it come to me. I don't have to make it happen or chase it. Mindfulness isn't meant to instantly solve my problems, but it does help me worry less about things." —Ben, age sixteen

You can tell yourself the same thing Ben did, or whatever works to remind yourself to stay patient and accepting when practicing mindfulness.

3. FEELING FRUSTRATED IF MINDFULNESS DOES NOT SEEM HELPFUL

It is easy to fall into the trap of believing that each mindful breath is supposed to relieve you of all your stress. Most of the time, it's true that mindfulness lessens the intensity of your worries and improves your mood. Bear in mind, however, your brain's tendency to be negative. According to psychologist Rick Hanson, our brains are like Velcro for negative experiences, but Teflon for positive ones. What he means by this is that negative thoughts seem to stick in our brains, whereas positive ones slip out as easily as food sliding off a nonstick pan.

The more you practice mindfulness, the more it will help you get past your mind's negativity, which is often rooted in the things you worry about. However, even seasoned mindfulness practitioners still need to manage their expectations. Being mindful does not totally vanquish worries and negative thoughts from your life. Some days, practicing mindfulness will feel more productive than others. For best results, you can focus on being a more mindful person in general rather than on getting perfect results when practicing mindful awareness. Accept frustration when it arises, and gently remind yourself that the benefits of mindfulness will come over time.

Teens in Their Own Words

"Pressuring myself to be worry free or happier during or after I practice mindfulness gets me discouraged. [So instead] I just [tell myself to] notice whatever I think and feel and not be attached to an outcome." —Alex, age fifteen

4. SEEING MINDFULNESS AS A CHORE

Do you love doing chores? My guess is probably not. That's because we see chores as work—something we have to do. If you're like most teens, and probably the grown-ups in your life too, you don't like being told what to do by anyone, even yourself!

Think about how annoyed you feel when you try to tell yourself not to eat something you are really craving, not to do what you really want to do, or not to go where you really want to go.

Mindfulness will feel more welcome and enjoyable to you if you think of it as a choice, not a chore. You certainly don't have to sit in a lotus position (legs crossed) and meditate for hours to experience the joys that mindfulness can bring. You can practice mindfulness for two hours, for twenty minutes, or for just a few minutes at a time. And you can do it anytime, anywhere, and with anyone. The more you practice mindfulness, of course, the better it will work for you.

Teens in Their Own Words

"I practice mindfulness because I want to—but not because I have to. Reminding myself that it calms me and makes me less upset helps me want to do it." —Tamika, age thirteen

---

5. SEEING MINDFULNESS AS A GOAL

Do you like to keep track of how well you are achieving by listing your accomplishments? Do you create a lot of to-do lists on paper or your mobile device and take pleasure in crossing off items? If so, or if you simply know that you're an achievement-oriented person, you may feel as though you are on a graded mission to mindfulness. Kind of as though you have to get an A in mindfulness and then you've mastered it.

Yet have you noticed that sometimes when you reach a goal you've set for yourself, the excitement fades pretty quickly? How long have you truly held on to a thought like *I'm feeling* great because I got a good grade, I really rocked that dance recital, or *I'm so pumped that I made the basketball team*? Sure, attaining these goals feels great, but they simply don't make you eternally happy.

It is good to strive for, and achieve, goals. (Just don't fall into the trap of basing your self-esteem on your achievements rather than your unique personal qualities.) But even if, one day, after practicing mindfulness you feel fantastic and totally worry-free—like, *I nailed it!*—mindfulness can help you only when you use it in the present moment. In other words, having been mindful in the past isn't going to help you worry less in the future. It's not like a "Get Out of Jail Free" card. But knowing how to be mindful, and using that knowledge by making mindfulness a healthy habit, will keep your worries in check.

Conner's Story

Many parts of seventeen-year-old Conner's life were filled with ongoing ambitions. He was striving to get decent grades, he actively participated in activities in and out of school, and he had strong ambitions for getting into a top college.

Conner kept his overarching desires for goals from sabotaging his mindfulness practice by doing some helpful self-talk. Whenever he started to feel pressure to reach a goal—to "get somewhere" by being mindful—he told himself, Just by noticing my breath, I am already there. *In other words, a moment of mindfulness is just the same as any other moment of mindfulness.*

Every time your turn your attention toward your breath, or notice distracting thoughts in a different way by not reacting to them, you're using mindfulness and letting go of your worries. Mindfulness is an all-or-nothing game. It's not something anyone can do better than anyone else, because at any given moment no one can do anything more mindful than notice their breath. Pretty amazing, huh? It can feel good to use mindfulness to give you a break from competing against others or yourself, to meet goals, or to win.

6. WANTING TO GIVE UP ON MINDFULNESS BECAUSE YOU STILL GET WORRIES

Given all the stresses in your life, you may feel like "throwing in the mindfulness towel" at times. If you remember the "Seeing You Can Let Go" exercise from the end of chapter 1, it likely helped you reflect on your ability to work through your past worries. The point was to notice your triumphs over things that you did or could have worried about. Similarly, teens tell me that it helps to keep them motivated to practice mindfulness if they remind themselves that mindfulness won't eradicate their worries.

Teens in Their Own Words

"I don't have to give up on mindfulness, even though I still get worried about some things. It helps to see these upsetting thoughts are just part of what I am thinking—they don't own me. Mindfulness is about me not judging myself on those tough days. No way am I giving up on that amazing reality check I get from practicing it." —Rob, age sixteen

Now that you know how acceptance can help you overcome obstacles to practicing mindfulness, let's look at how acceptance will reduce the power that those worry thoughts themselves, and the painful emotions that go with them, have over your mind.

Acceptance of Worries Helps You Let Them Go

So far we've discussed how acceptance gets you out from under thoughts that can create obstacles to learning and practicing mindfulness itself.

Now that I'm fairly certain you'll continue to give mindfulness a chance, let's talk about accepting worries and other troubling thoughts that are bound to cross your mind when you're practicing mindfulness. Mindfully accepting and managing your worries is like watching clouds float across the sky. Clouds may darken your view, but they come and they go: instead of getting caught up in the clouds, you can let them pass. Now let's go deeper into the power of acceptance for seeing your worries in a new way.

Broadening Your View of the World

The things you worry about, in all likelihood, are things you tend to view in a rigid and narrow way. For example, if you worry when you see a dog because you automatically think that all dogs are dangerous, you're not using your higher thinking to consider the fact that the vast majority of dogs are gentle, affectionate, and safe to be around. Or, maybe you are afraid to go to parties or other gatherings because you think that the people there will ignore you and that you'll feel self-conscious. Many teens with social anxiety, whose worries keep them from going out, tell me they feel upset about missing out on the fun of these social events. Yet they still resist going out, for fear of a negative experience.

The term "selective attention" refers to how our brains pay attention to only some of the many things to see in our environment. Worrying can make your attention even more selective, causing you to focus on things that seem to support your fears, making your worries stronger. For example, if you're worried that you'll be attacked by a dog, and you see a man walking a dog, you might not notice that the man has the dog on a short leash and that the dog is happily wagging its tail. You might notice only that the dog is large and has many sharp teeth. Acceptance helps us let go of worries because it gives us some mental distance from them so that we can pause to reflect, broaden our view of potential problems and challenges, and react to them in a different, healthier way.

Broadening Your View of Yourself

Given the fact that you're reading this book, you probably think of yourself as a worrier. Maybe people call you a "worry-wart," a "gloom and doom" person, or a pessimist, and you've come to identify with such labels. Or, if you had to describe yourself in five words, perhaps "worrier" would be one of them. If that's the case, then an attitude of acceptance can offer you a more freeing, positive way to view yourself and help you manage your worries at the same time.

Narrowly seeing yourself as a "worrier" is a form of selective attention whereby you see yourself in a limited and unhealthy way. The way you see yourself has a direct influence on your thoughts. If you self-identify as a "worrier," you're more likely to have worries, because it fits with your self-concept. You will subconsciously direct your thoughts to live up to the "worrier" label.

But with your newly learned attitude of acceptance, you can pause and shift the way you view yourself when worries arise. Instead of labeling yourself simply as a total worrier, you can begin to accept yourself as someone who worries at times or as someone who worries more often than you would like to. After all, everyone worries. Why should you be hard on yourself by labeling yourself as a "worrier"? In the field of counseling, there is a type of "talk therapy" called cognitive-behavioral therapy, in which people learn how to avoid negatively labeling themselves. The basic message of cognitive-behavioral therapy is that unfair, exaggerated, distorted thoughts are what feed anxiety, depression, and other negative emotional states.

Let's now turn to Jan, who created problems in her life by seeing herself as a worrier, which created a subconscious drive to live up to that label.

Teens in Their Own Words

"I had spent so much time worrying. You name it, and I found a way to worry about it. When I bought into that worrier label, I had made that my total identity. I really never thought I'd see myself as anything but a worrier. Mindfulness helped me realize that I felt stuck by labeling myself in this limited way. I learned that acceptance of my anxiety allowed me to feel more in control of how I see myself. I now have a choice to see myself as a person who worries, but that does not make me a total worrier. I don't have to limit my choices of what I do or where I go just because worries pop into my head." —Jan, age fifteen

Next is a mindfulness exercise, similar to what Jan effectively used, that consists of using your breath and welcoming acceptance for letting go of the "worrier" label and seeing your worries in a healthier way.

try this! Responding to Your Worries with Acceptance

Part 1

Find a quiet space, and close your eyes if you're comfortable doing so. Take three in-breaths, and with each out-breath say to yourself, Even though I have worries, this does not make me a worrier. Now take a few minutes to gently let yourself absorb this empowering statement. Don't judge how well it seems to be working. Just feel good about valuing yourself beyond your tendencies to worry.

Part 2

Get a sheet of paper and jot down some thoughts, make a list, or draw a picture to represent a new, broader way of seeing yourself than just as a worrier. What new activities can you pursue if you accept yourself in an expanded way and let go of seeing yourself as a "worrier"? How do you think that will that make you feel? How will seeing yourself in a broader way help you improve your relationships with others?

Given your brain's Velcro-like ability to hold on to negative thoughts, don't get discouraged if you slip back to seeing yourself as a "worrier." The last thing you want to do is beat yourself up. Instead, just revisit this exercise. Gently practice accepting the thought *I am a worrier.* Just because you think something doesn't mean it's true, but you can accept the thought nonetheless, without having to buy into it. Then shift to viewing yourself as a person who tends to worry at times and who knows how to cope by using the mindfulness skills you're learning.

Accepting That Worries Will Pass

If you have some jitters about a test to study for or a presentation to make, this is normal anxiety. Normal anxiety can motivate you to study for that test or prepare for that presentation. Making preparations is one of the best ways to cope with worries.

The problem is that worries can remain and bounce around in your head even though you are studying, preparing, or doing anything else to manage the challenges that come your way. These worries are counterproductive, and it is important that you not get caught up in them. Noticing and accepting

81

your worries as mere passing thoughts will create a wonderful, freeing shift in how you feel. This is what mindfulness is all about—staying in the present without getting tangled up in judging how you think or feel. Following are some visualization exercises that can help you react to your worries differently by reducing the impact that they have on you.

try this! Leaves Floating on a Stream

Imagine a flowing stream with leaves floating on the surface, carried gently by the current. Take a few seconds to really visualize the scene. Then, for the next few minutes, whenever a worry enters your mind, imagine placing it on a leaf. Let it float by. Just let this imaginary stream flow naturally. Don't speed up the current or try to get rid of the leaves. Notice your worries floating away from you at their own speed, whatever that may be. Being mindful is about gently letting go of worries and other thoughts at their own pace.

If your mind says *This is dumb* or *I can't do this*, place these thoughts on leaves, too, and let them pass. Watch the stream for a few seconds. If a leaf gets stuck, allow it to hang around until it's ready to float by. If the same thought comes up again, watch it float by another time. Watch the stream for a few seconds. If you feel bored, impatient, or frustrated, just say to yourself, *I notice having a feeling of boredom/impatience/frustration.* Place that thought on a leaf and allow it to float along too. Afterward, ask yourself what it was like to visualize your worries floating by on leaves. Did it feel liberating to not try to shove them away and just let them pass?

Now let's try a different kind of visualization for letting go of worries with mindfulness.

try this! Sitting on a Hill and Watching Cars Go By

Imagine sitting on top of a hill near a highway and watching the cars go by. Or imagine looking down on railroad cars moving along a track that stretches in each direction as far as you can see. As you see the cars go by, think of them as your worries, and just notice them as they pass. If one worry seems to appear over and over again, or it just won't pass, then say to yourself, *I accept that this is what I am thinking right now, and that's okay.*

Afterward, reflect on whether this exercise also helped you let go of worries. Did you feel the power that comes with not holding on to your worries and learning to let them go?

More Visualizations for Letting Go of Worry

The following brief visualization exercises give you more options for mindfully noticing and letting go of your worries. Follow the same process as for leaves floating on a stream or cars going by. Decide which imagery you like the most or which imagery works best for you. You can practice any of these visualizations for as long and as often as you want. (Some of these visualizations, such as blowing bubbles or skipping rocks, can be done in real life. Imagine letting go of your worries as you go through the physical motions. Just don't take a Sharpie and try to write on bees or actually jump onto an assembly-line conveyor belt!)

- Visualize bees going from flower to flower. When a worry comes up, imagine writing it on a bee, and watch it buzz around until it's out of sight.

- Visualize boxes moving along an assembly line. Mark each of your worries on a box with a big rubber stamp as it goes down the line.

- Imagine blowing bubbles with an oversize bubble wand. Each bubble holds a worry or a different kind of thought. Watch the bubbles float away.

- Imagine your worries on giant parade floats. Watch them pass you on the street and as they slowly shrink into the distance.

- Visualize yourself on a lakeshore, skipping rocks. Put each worry on a rock, throw it, and watch it bounce along before it sinks.

- Picture your worries as images popping up and fading away on a digital screen.

Eric's Story

Eric, age sixteen, felt attached to the "worrier" label, just like Jan (who was discussed earlier). Eric felt the breathing exercise that Jan used was helpful, but he wanted something he could picture in his mind. He experimented and found that a variation of the leaves on a stream exercise gave him a really good visual way to let go of his "worrier" label. It went like this:

*He imagined leaves with the label of "worrier" floating
away in a stream. Next he imagined a new leaf falling to
the ground from a nearby tree. He visualized picking it up
and symbolically turning over this new leaf and noticing its
uniqueness with beginner's mind. Then he said out loud the
message that was written on his new leaf. "I am no longer a
worrier. When I do tend to worry, I can use my mindfulness
skills to let my worries go."*

Like Eric, you too can create your own variations of the
mindfulness exercises that you find helpful. Let's now combine
mindful breathing with a visualization of a "higher level" as
a way for you to free yourself of worries. I have been using
the following exercise with my teen clients for many years. (An
audio version is available at www.newharbinger.com/39812.)

try this! Floating on a Soft, White, Fluffy Cloud

Imagine that you are floating on a white, soft, fluffy cloud. Feel the sun
gently warming your body. Now breathe in, feeling your body gently
rise a few inches as you do so. And as you breathe out and slowly
sink back down, let your worries and stress float away from your body,
through the cloud, and into the surrounding air.

Afterward, how did it feel to float on the cloud? Did you feel physically and emotionally lighter? Was it helpful to visualize letting your
worries leave your body?

Opening Your Heart to Gratitude

Every teen can think of something to be thankful for, no
matter how many worries they have in their lives. For example,

Doug, age thirteen, shared with me how much it meant to him when his friends remembered his birthday. Alyssa, age fourteen, warmly reflected how much she appreciated her mother taking her to junior high cheerleading meets and preparing all the refreshments for the squad. On a more fundamental level, Brock, age fifteen, had a new appreciation for living in a developed country after he learned in his social studies class that in many countries people don't have clean water or enough food. What do these teens' reflections have in common? They're all about feeling gratitude.

The more you bring gratitude into your life and mindfully focus on it, the less you will focus on your worries. Gratitude goes hand in hand with mindfulness. When you take the time to notice, accept, and reflect on your experience, you'll have the opportunity to appreciate how fortunate you are, either when something good happens or simply in general. Being grateful on a regular basis can have a huge positive effect on your life. People who often feel grateful and appreciative are happier, less stressed, and less depressed. At a time when you might be worried about something that you missed or something that you think you'll never have, gratitude will focus you on all that you *do* have—turning the tables on those negative thoughts.

Have you ever gotten new hiking boots and, while wearing them around, been surprised at how many other people are wearing a similar kind of boots? Or have you ever not noticed just how common a certain kind of car was until your family bought one too? It's not that suddenly more people are wearing the kind of shoes you just got or that more people are driving that make and model of car; it's that you're noticing these things more because you're subconsciously on the lookout for things that validate your choices. Similarly, if you make the choice to have an attitude of gratitude, you'll start to see more and more things out there to be grateful for. You'll remember to slow down and notice what's around you. For example, you'll step outside and think: *Wow, the sky is beautiful today! What an incredible world we live in.* Or you'll see an acquaintance and think: *There's Sara! It was so nice of her to help me yesterday.*

Noticing the things you're grateful for will help you build a gratitude habit. I encourage you to do the following gratitude exercise to experience a wonderful new way of looking at your life, a way that can help you feel more at the center of everything that's going on.

try this! Take a Gratitude Shower

Too often we focus on things in life we want and don't have. This can leave us feeling empty and miserable and trigger us to worry about whether better circumstances will come our way. By focusing more on what you are grateful for in your life, you'll feel less stressed out because you'll feel more fulfilled. Simply close your eyes and picture the "good stuff" in your life streaming down on you. Notice how satisfying it feels to notice the things in your life that you are grateful for. For example, you can be thankful that you have eyes to read or ears to listen. Perhaps you are grateful for your family, your friends, or having fun interests in your life. As you notice all the great things in your life, your gratitude shower may take longer than you expected because you see even more "good stuff" now that you are opening yourself to noticing it. Hey, this is your imaginary mindfulness exercise, and since nobody is watching you, go ahead and stretch out and dance around in your gratitude shower! (And, here is some really good news: teens have never once told me that their parents complain that they are taking too long in this kind of shower!)

There is nothing wrong with wanting improvements in your life—as long as you don't get too hung up on what you don't have. Now that you've taken a gratitude shower, can you see how being grateful leaves you feeling emotionally fulfilled, whereas being worried leaves you feeling emotionally empty and depleted?

Acceptance Supports Self-Compassion

We have discussed how accepting yourself without judgment is an important part of mindfulness for managing worries. This is closely related to the concept of self-compassion, which is about nurturing yourself when you're worried, upset, or otherwise emotionally hurting.

Kristin Neff, the founder of the self-compassion movement, points out how we instinctively tend to be really good at giving compassion to the people we value (that is, the people we care about). Think about your best friends. Have you ever comforted a friend who was worried that she had failed a test? If so, you likely said something supportive, such as "Hey, you probably did well, but, if not, you'll do better next time." Imagine one day the same friend tearfully tells you she just got dumped and is worried what people will think. Being compassionate, you might say: "I know you'll get through this, I've got your back, and I'm here to listen. You have a lot to offer, and no gossip can ever take away from how awesome you are as a person."

When it comes to the way we treat *ourselves*, it's a different story. Frequently, we are really just too hard on ourselves. Not showing yourself the same compassion you'd offer a friend can buy you a one-way ticket to worry wasteland. Let's say you wish you had done something differently, or you have harsh thoughts that what you did or are about to do is wrong. Instead of forgiving yourself and moving on, you punish yourself by worrying, as though you're not allowed to make mistakes.

Self-compassion can help you stay out of worry wasteland by stopping you from using worries to be hard on yourself. Consider that most people are really good about encouraging others to not put themselves down and to worry less. Even though we can instinctively serve up heaps of compassion for others, we tend to resist or totally neglect giving it to ourselves. By embracing self-compassion for ourselves, however, we can learn to focus our attention on soothing and taking care of ourselves when we feel worried. Try the self-compassion exercises below to start putting more self-compassion into your life and seeing how it can help you manage your worries.

try this! Gaining Acceptance Through Self-Compassion

The following exercise is inspired by the excellent self-compassion work of Kristin Neff.

1. **Think about the ways that worries can cause you to beat yourself up.** Let's say you worry that you come on too strong with strangers, that you're not working hard enough in school, or that you're gaining weight. Do you think beating yourself up over it will make you change things for the better? If so, take a few breaths and reflect on how being critical toward yourself fuels your worries. Remind yourself that you don't have to be perfect. Let go of your self-criticism, gently embracing com-

passion for yourself by resolving to learn from your mistakes and accepting that everyone experiences setbacks.

2. Now, letting go of beating yourself up for your shortcomings, move forward with intention to change something about yourself, if you desire. How would it feel to be more accepting of yourself and not dwell on your shortcomings? Probably as if a huge weight had been lifted off your shoulders. How would shedding your harsh self-judgments and worries allow you to improve socially, academically, and in other ways? I bet you would feel less hesitant and more sure of yourself when hanging out with others or when going to apply effort in school or outside activities. With that in mind, come up with some supportive words to motivate yourself to stay positive. One teen client taught me three such words, which I hold on to closely: "Know your value!" Another teen told me she felt supportive of herself by saying, "I try my best, and if I make mistakes they are great learning opportunities."

Now try another self-compassion-based exercise that involves healthy self-love. Literally embracing yourself will help you soothe, forgive, and reassure yourself when you're worried that things aren't going so well in your life. Learning to mindfully hug yourself in a self-calming, nurturing way will help you feel emotionally stronger when you're super stressed out. This exercise also provides a nice transition to mindfully focusing on your body, which is the emphasis of the next chapter.

try this! Self-Acceptance Hug for Self-Compassion

Take a few mindful breaths. On your next in-breath, stretch your arms out wide and then bring them in for a big, firm self-hug. Now loosen your arms across your shoulders as you breathe out and then re-embrace yourself more firmly on your next in-breath. Repeat this a few times.

Afterward, reflect on how it felt to warmly accept and nurture yourself in this gentle, caring, affirming way. What does this tell you about your ability to comfort yourself?

In this chapter, you learned how to be mindful when you're doubting your ability to do so or when you're just "not feeling it." It is crucial that you not let your distracting thoughts, misperceptions, and negative judgments convince you to give mindfulness the boot. Thus, acceptance of whatever thoughts go through your mind, including negative ones about mindfulness, is key to staying the course. You learned that viewing your worries with an accepting attitude is a great way to disarm them and feel less stressed out by them. In addition, you now know about visualizations, gratitude, and self-compassion, which are valuable tools for welcoming and keeping mindfulness in your life.

Here's what teens have said about the benefits of using acceptance to help them let go of worries.

Teens in Their Own Words

"With mindfulness, I am not getting as stressed out anymore. The things I worry about are still there, but I don't freak out about them like I used to." —Travon, age thirteen

"My best friend said mindfulness helps her let go of things that bother her. That sounded cool, so I am trying mindfulness exercises, and they are helping me accept my life as it is and calm down too." —Rosa, age fifteen

"Accepting that I may not get a perfect grade led me to realize that it also won't make me broke and homeless." —Duane, age sixteen

"My days feel sooo much easier when I remind myself that I can't control everything that I worry about." —Shelly, age eighteen

So far, we've been discussing mindfulness as something that goes on in your mind. In the next chapter, we'll look at mindfulness for your body.

chapter 5

mindfulness for your body

The organs weep the tears the eyes refuse to shed.

—Sir William Osler

This quote from William Osler, an 18th-century physician, refers to the fact that suppressed emotions can result in physical illnesses. In much the same way, the stress caused by our minds' worries often finds a home in our bodies. When you worry, your body reacts by becoming tense. This tension can manifest in various ways—for example, headache, stomachache, nausea, rash, dizziness, or fatigue—as mentioned in chapter 1. Have you ever experienced any of the following physical symptoms or bodily signals when you were worried (or just as you started to worry)?

- Rapid breathing

- Headache

- Queasiness (stomach butterflies)

- Back or neck ache

- Dry mouth

- Stomachache

- Sweaty palms

- Flushed or hot cheeks

- Fast heartbeat

- Feeling tired

- Inability to concentrate

- Feeling weak

- Trembling

- Loss of appetite

- Sleep problems

- Cramps

If so, the following quotes from teens who worry show that you're certainly not alone.

Teens in Their Own Words

"I sat down to take that test and my head was pounding, I knew I was going to fail." —Barry, age fourteen

"Oh wow, I'm shaking. I must really be worried."
—Tammy, age fifteen

"When I get really worried, I feel like I'm gonna throw up!"
—Barbara, age sixteen

"I've been so stressed out and worried, now I'm totally exhausted." —Chet, age seventeen

"I get these red blotches on my neck when I am really worried, and then I feel self-conscious." —Heather, age nineteen

In this chapter, you will learn:

- How physical symptoms can result from, or worsen from, worrying

- Your specific physical reactions, discomfort, and pain in response to worrying

- How your bodily reactions to worry can lead you to worry even more

- How to calm your body and relax your mind

By becoming more mindful of your body, you'll be able to tune in to its important messages. Using mindfulness strategies and tools to manage your body's reactions to the stress that comes from worrying will reduce the overall frequency of your worries, just like the other mindfulness practices you have learned so far.

The Mind-Body Connection

Your mind and your body are strongly connected. Given this powerful association, it is really important that you train both your mind and your body to work well together to manage worries. Mindfulness is as much about tuning in to your body as it is about being aware of what's going on in your mind. This makes mindfulness valuable for looking after both your emotional and your physical health.

When you shift your attention to acknowledging your body sensations with mindfulness, you'll naturally be drawn to the here and now. When you think of right now, you can't think of yesterday or tomorrow, so any worries about what may have happened or what might happen won't be able to get ahold of your attention. Mindfulness of your body is, therefore, a wonderful way to get your mind off your worries!

Your body, like your breath, is a natural anchor for mindfulness, when you pay attention to it. Becoming mindful of your body means accepting its signals—for example, muscle tension or achiness—without judgment, rather than reacting to or ignoring them. Noticing your body in this special way will help you release the stress that can inhabit different parts of it as a result of your worries.

What Is Happening Within Your Body

Worrying takes a toll on your body, and the resulting stress signals can, in turn, prompt you to worry even more. If you tend to experience physical symptoms (like the teens quoted at the beginning of this chapter) when you worry, these symptoms themselves likely give you cause for concern. The more concerned you get about the sensations in your body (not to mention your concern about whether people can see that you're worried, especially if you have social anxiety), the more your mind has to worry about. This can lead to an unhealthy cycle of being too absorbed in your body and letting it influence your mind. The following illustration shows how worried thoughts influence your body's reactions and how these reactions, in turn, can lead to more worries.

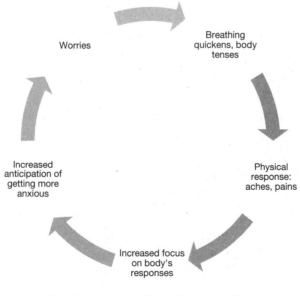

The Worried Mind-Body Reaction Cycle

As you can see, worries can affect your mind and body in a way that makes you more upset. Let's now take a closer look at how when worries get stuck in your head, they can create aches, pains, and other problems in your body.

Worries Come at a Cost, and Your Body Pays the Price

As mentioned in chapter 1, when your "primitive, reacting brain" kicks out worries, very often these worries are false alarms. Most of the things you worry will happen (your "What ifs") aren't likely to happen. Nevertheless, those worries shift your body into stress mode, as though a disaster is about to happen and you need to be ready for it. Therefore, when you worry that you'll fail an upcoming test, your chest feels tight. When you worry that you'll be a lifelong social outcast, you get butterflies in your stomach. Or when you worry that you won't succeed in college, your head starts to pound. These are all real worries and symptoms that teens have shared with me.

That old "reacting brain" creates the "fight, flight, or freeze" reaction, which is what drives these worry-related bodily reactions (pounding in your chest or head, tension in your body, and all-around unpleasant jitters). Mindfulness gives you the choice to notice these bodily reactions to worries in a less intense, calmer way. This helps your "fight, flight, or freeze" bodily responses subside much more quickly. And, with practice, it helps them not arise in the first place. This is why mindfulness is good not only for your mind but also for your body.

Mindfulness Changes the Worry Mind-Body Reaction Cycle

Mindfulness stops the cycle of worried mind and stressed body by changing how you respond. As we've discussed, when you practice mindfulness, you're not trying to "get rid" of anything going on in your head, including those pesky worries. That same idea applies to learning to mindfully notice, without judgment, what's going on in your body.

By experiencing your physical sensations with an accepting attitude, you can calm your body's reaction to worries.

Corrine's Story

Corrine, age seventeen, had been getting migraine headaches ever since the beginning of her junior year of high school. When she first came to me for counseling, she said that her parents, teachers, and friends had repeatedly told her, "It is your junior year now, and you have to do really well!" Understandably, she was feeling a lot of pressure to get good grades.

Nothing seemed to help with her headaches, and that scared her. Not only was she having these really bad headaches, she was starting to dread them. She would get majorly worried about when the next one was going to happen. She had already seen her family doctor and two different neurologists in search of help. So, in counseling with me, she had nothing to lose by trying mindfulness...

Read on, and later I'll tell you what Corrine had to say after she experienced the power of mindfulness and the mind-body connection.

Practicing Mindfulness for Your Body

To start using mindfulness to help you manage your body's reactions to worries, try the following exercises. We'll begin with shorter exercises to help you get tuned in to your body. We'll finish with the body scan, which is an in-depth, powerful, core mindfulness experience. Some of these exercises may feel more helpful than others, and that's okay, but I hope you'll give each one a chance.

The acronym RAIN, first coined by Michele McDonald, is an easy-to-remember tool for practicing mindfulness. RAIN stands for:

(R) Recognize

(A) Allow

(I) Inquire and investigate

(N) Not totally defining yourself (The exercise will explain.)

RAIN promotes recognizing, allowing, investigating, and not identifying with the sensations you feel in your body as a result of worry (or as a result of anything else, for that matter). When it comes to being mindful of what is going on in your body, you will find it helpful to be in the RAIN.

try this! Noticing Your Body in the RAIN

Approach this RAIN exercise and all others in this book with a beginner's mind of being curious and accepting of whatever the RAIN feels like to you. Keep a flexible mind-set for how long you stay in the RAIN. I suggest that you spend a few minutes in each of the four steps. If, however, you move through some steps slower or faster than others, that is okay too. Know that the gentle, nonjudgmental part of mindfulness is something you can stay in touch with—even in the RAIN.

(R) Recognize: Take a few deep breaths, and focus your attention on your body. How is your body feeling right now? Try to recognize what's going on beneath the surface as well as at the surface (your skin). Is your body sending you signals of any sort? Are there any areas where you notice feeling tense? Any areas where you notice feeling relaxed? Do any parts of your body feel warm or cold? Are you experiencing any pressure sensations or pain?

(A) Allow: Allow the sensations in your body to be there. If you feel an urge to yawn or scratch an itch, just notice it and most likely it will go away. Don't judge any bodily sensations as good or bad. Don't dwell on what they might mean. Just accept that they're present right now, without trying to fight or suppress them.

(I) Inquire and Investigate: Ask yourself whether the sensations in your body are familiar or whether they're new to you. Try to feel a deep awareness of each sensation, observing how it changes or moves over time.

(N) Not Totally Defining Yourself: Notice the sensations in your body as just one part of your overall being. These sensations have not *always* been with you. You won't continue to experience these exact same sensations *forever*. The fact is, they're simply passing through. They're not an enduring part of who you are. You're not stuck with

101

them. You are more than the feelings in your body. Think about that for a while.

What sensations, if any, did you notice in your body? How did it feel to notice your bodily sensations without judgment? Did RAIN help lessen your focus on your worries, or can you see how it might help you in the future?

Next, you'll mindfully travel to the parts of your body that make contact with the ground or contact with the furniture you're on. Being mindful of where your body makes contact with your surroundings will gently lead your worrying mind and tense body to a calmer place. The second aspect of the exercise is gratitude. Simple gratitude for feeling physically supported, whether you're standing, sitting, or lying down, can also ease your worries.

try this! Connecting with Your Body Through Contact

You can do this exercise indoors or outdoors. A recommended position is sitting in a comfortable chair or on a comfy pillow or gently leaning against a tree or the side of your house or a building.

1. Take a few calming breaths.

2. Notice at least three points where your body makes contact with itself or the surfaces around you. If you are sitting down, you can think about your body touching the chair you are sitting in as well as parts of your body in contact with itself. If you are lying down, then notice where your body is in contact with that surface. Pick three points of contact.

3. Reflect on how your body feels at these three points. If there is a sense of pressure, where do you feel it? Is there comfort? Is there pain? What parts of your body feel relaxed?

4. Notice this experience for a few minutes.

Discovering What Is Going on Inside You

Now let's focus less on what is going on the surface of your body and more on what is happening within it. We all have numerous sensations going on in our bodies at any given time. Most of the time, we are not that tuned in to them. Check out the exercise below and take the opportunity to notice what is going on inside your body. You may find it similar to RAIN, but perhaps you will notice some differences. Seventeen-year-old Keisha, when exploring her inner sensations, shared, "This exercise gets me out of my head by refocusing on what is going on inside my body." Keisha saw this exercise as a wonderful anchor to help her feel grounded and less uptight.

try this! Exploring Sensations Within

Gently take three in-breaths and out-breaths. Notice three sensations in your body right now. If you notice more than three, that is fine too. Count them on your fingers, or, if you prefer, in your mind.

Afterward, how was the experience of reflecting on where these sensations are? What was it like to just notice them and sit with the feelings?

Now we are literally going to "move on" to another helpful mindfulness exercise: walking meditation.

Is your walk along the way to and from school such a dull routine that you don't pay attention to your surroundings? Perhaps your body seems to move all on its own, leaving your mind free to become filled with worries. Or maybe it feels so boring that your mind seems to detach from your body and float away.

Walking meditation is exactly the opposite of this. It involves simply being mindful and being connected with your body when you are walking. By focusing on the movement of your feet, and every other part of your body, you move "out of your head" (so to speak) and into your body. You get in touch with what an amazingly complicated machine your body is. Being tuned into your body through mindful walking will really help to clear those worries from your mind.

You can walk mindfully pretty much anywhere or anytime. For informal walking meditation, just notice your breathing, how your arms move as you walk, and how the rest of your body moves along as well. Be free and flexible, varying your stride length and speed as you move you to where you are going. Take in your surroundings with increased awareness of what you see, hear, smell, and feel as you walk along. Or, you can do walking meditation as a formal activity, as described below.

try this! Getting Your Mind and Body in Step Through Walking Meditation

Walking meditation as a formal practice is a more measured experience, but, even so, you can do it in the setting of your choice. Before you start your formal mindful walking session, decide where you would like to be walking. You can plan out a route in a room of your house, in your backyard, in a community park, or along a hiking path. It doesn't have to be long. Teens tell me that even three to five minutes of walking meditation gets them out of worry wasteland. After you have done it a few times, you may want to do longer formal walking meditations of five to ten minutes or even longer, if that feels good to you.

Once you are at your desired location, spend a minute or two just standing there, breathing deeply and anchoring your attention in your body. Some teens prefer to walk in a straight line and then turn around, walking back and forth in this fashion. Other teens tell me they like the feeling of walking in a circle. You can try out different options and do what feels preferable.

As you walk, notice your feet, notice what your senses are taking in, and check out your immediate surroundings. To maximize your ability to focus, I encourage you to deliberately walk as slowly and silently as possible for the full duration of your formal mindful walking activity. Now begin to take two or three mindful steps as slowly and silently as possible. Continue to walk deliberately slowly as you mindfully notice the sensations in the bottoms of your feet and throughout your body as it moves. Teens generally tell me they prefer to keep their eyes open and gaze slightly downward to best focus on the experience of their walking. Notice what you see, smell, hear, and feel as you walk. You can briefly close your eyes at times (if it's safe to do so). If you find yourself getting distracted by thoughts and worries, just accept the distractions and gently return your focus to your feet. Simply notice the experience of your alternating steps.

The body scan is another wonderful exercise to re-center your worried mind, bringing it back to the here and now. The body scan involves focusing on different parts of your body, one at a time. It's a way to appreciate your own body. Because we live in a body-critical culture and you're still developing, you may think your body leaves much to be desired. But your body is unique and has a lot of cool parts. Your body does a lot for you every day. By focusing on your body with beginner's mind, and connecting to it in a more mindful way than usual, you will truly notice how awesome your whole body really is! Valuing your body from the inside is a way to feel love and compassion for yourself, as well as to feel calm and relaxed, which will help with your worries. (We discuss cultivating a positive body image further in chapter 7.)

try this! The Body Scan

Familiarize yourself with the body scan by reading the instructions below. Then record yourself reading the instructions and play it back, or download and listen to the audio version at http://www.newharbinger.com/39812. Another option is to have a partner (such as a friend or family member) read the instructions out loud while you do the body scan and then switch roles to take turns.

Before you begin the body scan, you may want to make sure you're wearing loose-fitting, comfortable clothing, to help you feel relaxed and to better tune in to your internal sensations rather than the feeling of your clothes. I also recommend you remove your shoes. As you scan your body, you may notice sensations such as discomfort, tension, aches, pains, coldness, or stiffness. You may also notice the opposite: soothing sensations, muscle relaxation, warmth, or looseness. You may also notice that parts of your body feel energized, while other parts feel tired. Or you may notice no sensations at all. What's cool about the body scan is that you don't have to feel pressure to say it works. There's no goal other than noticing the sensations in your body in a new way. But by tuning into your body without judgment, you'll likely feel calmer because you're not focused on your worries.

Let's begin.

1. Go to a place where you can comfortably lie down on your back—for example, on your bed, a soft carpet, or a mat. Keep your arms by your sides, palms facing up, legs gently apart, and close your eyes if that feels comfortable.

   Some teens tell me they feel more comfortable placing a pillow under their knees or just raising their knees in a bent position. Feel free to experiment with your position—you may even prefer to sit up.

2. Gently start bringing awareness to your body. Notice your body on the surface you're lying on, without judging whether your body feels lighter or heavier than normal.

   Notice the places your body is touching. Also notice, perhaps as you breathe out, a sense of yourself gently sinking a little deeper into the mat, bed, or chair.

3. Notice how your breath feels, including its movement within your body as you breathe in and out.

   Feel the warmth of your breath as it enters and exits your nose. Notice your chest or belly rising and falling. Continue being gently aware of your breath for a few minutes. Just know it is normal for your mind to wander during the body scan. When it does, gently refocus on your breath.

4. When you're ready, shift your focus to your left leg, moving all the way down your leg to below your big toe.

   Notice the sensations in your toes with a new sense of curiosity. Move your attention to your big toe, your little toe, and then the rest of your toes. What do they feel like? Do they tingle, not seem noticeable, or feel different in some other way? Are they tight or loose, or warm or cold?

As you breathe, imagine gently sending your breath down your body and into your toes.

As you breathe out, imagine your breath going back up your body and out through your nose. Apply this way of moving your breath to each part of your body.

Now move your awareness to the bottom of your foot. Notice the ball and heel. Does either feel heavy or light? As you move your attention to the sides and upper part of your left foot and ankle, pay attention to the sensations you feel in these areas. Draw your breath into all parts of your left foot. As you become aware of these sensations, gently let them go when you feel ready.

5. Move to the lower part of your left leg, knee, and upper leg, continuing to bring in the same intention of gentle, curious, accepting awareness.

6. In noticing your left leg in this special way, feel how the sensations in it may seem different than those in your right leg.

7. Gently shift your awareness up and down your right leg, extending down to your toes with a similar path of traveling awareness and then moving back up to your upper leg in the same way as you did with your left. Then let it go.

8. Now tune in to your pelvis area, hips, and buttocks. Notice what this area of your body feels like.

9. Move up to your lower torso, lower abdomen, and lower back.
Notice how your belly feels as you breathe in and out. Welcome in any emotions you feel here. Greet these gut feelings by exploring and accepting them as they are.

10. Gently shift your attention to your chest and upper back.

    Notice and feel your rib cage rising and falling, with a sense of curiosity, as you breathe in and out. Tune in to the beating of your heart. If you can, notice any emotions you are experiencing. Feel grateful for all the surrounding vital organs that are keeping you alive. Allow for any of your emotions that arise to express themselves.

11. Move your focus to both of your arms, beginning with your fingertips and moving up to your shoulders.

    Continue to breathe into and out of each body part before you move to the next one.

12. Gently move your awareness to your neck.

    After noticing your neck in this special way, move your awareness to your facial muscles, including your jaw, which often holds a lot of worry-related tension. Just notice whether this area feels tight or loose.

13. Move your awareness to the rest of your head, nonjudgmentally noticing it in this special way.

14. Gently send your breath up and down your body from your head and to your feet, and vice versa. Notice your breath as it freely travels within you, moving up and down your body. Feel the centering energy by letting your breath flow within you in this way.

15. Just let yourself be as you are. Just rest and relax for a few minutes in this gentle, peaceful place you have discovered within yourself.

Now that you've done the body scan, reflect on how you felt as you were doing it. Did you want to continue noticing your body in this special way, or did you start to feel bored? Are you feeling lighter, happier, less stressed out, or filled with energy? Are you pleased with the way you felt during and after the body scan, or are you disappointed with the experience? Regardless of the outcome, can you feel proud and grateful for giving yourself the opportunity to notice your body in this special way?

Starting with your toes and moving up to your head is the most popular way of doing the body scan, but in the future you can reverse the order if you prefer to. One colleague of mine starts with her head, claiming it helps relax her mind better, and then she works down to her toes.

The body scan, and the special awareness you get from it, is always available for you to revisit and reexperience. Each time you do it will likely feel a little different, depending on what's going on with you that day. By noticing your body without judgment, you'll learn to manage all sorts of bodily discomfort and to lessen any physical pain that you're feeling as a result of your worries. Teens tell me that the body scan also helps them see the connections between their emotions and physical sensations, which is key to overall health. I hope you give this wonderful exercise a fair chance. Remember that one of the beautiful things about mindfulness is that you don't have to judge the process or the results. Just patiently observe them as best as you can.

Let's return to Corrine, who, as you learned earlier in the chapter, was troubled by headaches, and see what she had to say after practicing mindfulness of her body.

Teens in Their Own Words

"Mindfulness actually helped me notice really *cool* sensations in my body that I never even knew were there. I also learned when my stress levels over school were getting way out of hand. By paying attention to my body in this different way, the stress lightened, and—unbelievable as this sounds—I get fewer headaches. When I do get them, they are not as bad."
—Corrine, age seventeen

In this chapter, you learned about the strong connection between your mind and your body. You also saw how a healthy awareness of your body can help your mind manage your worries. Now you can better recognize how the stress from worrying inhabits your body. And when you notice the impact of worries on your body, you can use mindfulness skills to notice your symptoms in a less reactive way. Practicing these body-oriented exercises on a regular basis, along with the other mindfulness practices we have covered so far, is one more way to lessen your worries.

Congratulations on learning the basics of mindfulness! In the next part of this book, you will use your new awareness and skills to learn how to cope with many common worries faced by teens, so that you may deal with future stressors mindfully.

PART 2

Mindfully Managing the Top Four Teen Worries

chapter 6

freeing yourself from school pressures

Teacher:	You did not send in your homework assignment last night, and now it is officially late!
Student:	My computer froze up last night.
Teacher:	So what does this mean for getting it done?
Student:	How about you give me a pass to go home, warm it back up, and I'll get back to you on that?

If your worries about school get in the way of doing work, be assured you're not alone. Though some students may be good at hiding it, most of your peers struggle with worries about school. School is filled with big-time pressures that teens have told me can really take them to worry wasteland.

For example, Jared, a struggling high-school senior, found his classes and homework super challenging. He was worried about getting enough credits to graduate. In contrast, Melissa, age sixteen, wanted to maintain her 4.3 grade point average (including weighted credits for her advanced placement classes) in hopes of getting into Harvard. Sienna, age fourteen, had switched to a public high school after years of being in private school. She was worried that the work may be different and harder in public school. Miguel, age thirteen, wanted to do really well in middle school to be eligible to for advanced classes in high school.

Excessive school-related worry often leads to panic that makes it hard for teens to meet challenges or to adapt when faced with setbacks. And school-related worries can really take a toll on your body. Corrine, as you may recall from chapter 5, had headaches related to school stress. Stomachaches are also a common ailment when teens become sick from worrying about school. In short, school-related worries can leave you feeling physically ill and emotionally drained. The emotional upset of school-related worries has resulted in some teens:

- isolating themselves from their peers and withdrawing from activities that used to give them pleasure;

- experiencing sudden mood fluctuations and intense emotions (for example, going from feeling very angry to crying); or

- engaging in self-destructive behaviors such as drug use, cutting, and binge eating or other forms of disordered eating.

Such physical and behavioral symptoms of school-related worry can ultimately affect how well you do in school, as well as your general health. So if you grew up thinking that you *need* to worry about school in order to get things done, to get good grades, to stay "on track" to succeed, or to have a bright future, you can see that worrying may not be such a good idea after all.

In this chapter, you will gain valuable tools for dealing with the stresses of school in a mindful way. We will draw from the mindfulness skills you've already been practicing and add some new ones. We will also weave in some cognitive-behavioral therapy strategies. We'll talk about how to handle some specific causes of school-related worry: distorted thinking, procrastination, and "What ifs." Then, we'll wrap up the chapter with some tips to help you mindfully tackle anxiety-causing homework, tests, and presentations (such as the dreaded oral report).

Some teens' biggest school-related worries have to do with difficult teachers and demanding class schedules. For other teens, extracurricular activities are a major source of worry. Some teens have to deal with tremendous parental pressure. Others experience anxiety over their difficulties with math, science, language arts, or social studies. Everyone has certain strengths and weaknesses when it comes to school. School-related worries are thus often very different from one teen to the next, and likely only you know what troubles you most often. With that in mind, here are some strategies to help you with school-related worry in general. Remember to keep an open and accepting attitude as you do the exercises.

Mindfulness for All School-Related Worries

Remember how breathing was introduced in chapter 2 as your trusty brake pedal to slow your racing mind? When you feel worried about school pressures, gently remind yourself that you will feel calmer with mindful breathing.

try this! Breathing in Calmness, Breathing Out School Worries

You can use this mindful breathing exercise any time you feel worried about school. Some teens I work with who have a lot of anxiety about school use it every weekday right after they wake up. Others use it when beginning classwork at school or doing homework after a long school day. I realize you may feel resistant to practicing mindful breathing, even briefly, amid your morning rush or after you feel like you just want to chill out with an electronic device or veg in front of the TV after a long school day. Just keep in mind, however, that even a brief mindfulness exercise will likely help tame your school stress and worries and can save you a lot of time that you'd end up wasting in worry wasteland. Yes, I know, those school days can really drag sometimes, and you probably wish you could just relax when you get home, instead of doing more work. But you may be amazed at what a difference this exercise really makes to calm your school stress and worries.

As you breathe in, empower yourself to feel calmness. Then imagine your school-related worries leaving you as you breathe out. For maximum effect, silently remind yourself that you're breathing in and out and tell yourself what you are trying to achieve in a few simple statements. Try these:

- *Breathing in, I am feeling calmer.*

- *Breathing out, I am releasing my fears and worries about school.*

- *Breathing in, I breathe in new energy.*

- *Breathing out, I release tiring school stress.*

Repeat three to five times.

By breathing mindfully, you create a pause in your mind to widen the space between your worried thoughts and your natural tendency to dwell on them. You unlock your thinking brain (see chapter 1), which allows you to see school pressures as just that—pressures. Then you have the choice of how best to deal with them.

Here's another exercise that teens say really helps them keep worried thoughts about school from dominating their attention. An audio version is available at http://www.newhar binger.com/39812.

try this! Floating School-Related Worries Downstream

Think of your worries about school as leaves floating past you in a stream. Visualize placing the stress of homework assignments, tests, projects, or that nerve-wracking presentation on those leaves, and watch them float away. As the stress related to these demands floats away, picture in their place helpful stepping-stones that will allow you to cross that stream of upsetting worries. Reflect on how much better you will feel about yourself as you move over each stepping stone, move past your worries that drifted away, and then take action to complete your work.

You don't need to worry to achieve in school, or for that matter, in any part of your life. Sadly, many teens confuse worrying about their immediate school demands and their future with caring about it. The gentle spirit and compassion of mindfulness allows for a distinction between caring and worrying. See the following table.

Worrying About School	Caring About School
Promotes fear and heightened anxiety	Encourages steady, consistent commitment
Leads to avoiding school work and homework	Supports motivation and engagement in tasks
Results in cramming for tests and panic	Leads to a focus on learning the material as you go
Causes you to have sleepless nights	Helps you rest and still do your best

You can replace your emotionally draining worries about school with the empowering awareness that comes with caring about it in a healthier way. Sure, worries about school will tend to pop up in your head at times. But with a gentle attitude shift, you can still care without needing to worry.

try this! Shifting from Worrying to Caring About School

Take a few mindful breaths and reflect on which school subjects and demands you most worry about.

Reflect on the benefits from shifting to a caring attitude instead of worrying about these school pressures. Take a few deep breaths and close your eyes and visualize clouds comprised of school-related worries floating off and fading away. Okay, imagine now that you are feeling grounded by standing on top of a large, level, and solid rock representing your caring energy. Notice how this rock both elevates you and centers you. Feel the sturdiness of this caring energy from the large rock you are standing on. Whenever you feel shaky in your confidence for school, this rock of caring is here to steady you while letting go of school worries and seeing them drift away with the clouds.

Mindfulness skills are crucial for quieting your racing thoughts and slowing you down to face the tasks you need to accomplish. But once you've done that, you may find yourself wondering *What should I do first?* Teens tell me they often feel lost or overwhelmed when trying to begin schoolwork or homework. Thus, another helpful and important part of practicing mindfulness for worries about school is to focus on setting a positive intention for success. Intention is all about knowing, at a deep level, *why* you're doing something. It can help give you a clear sense of priorities so that you can align your focus with what you want to get done.

try this! Setting a Positive Caring Intention for School Success

Focus on your breathing and relax. Set up a positive intention for school by saying to yourself. "Valuing myself means appreciating success in school. I am going to be present to study this information and retain it. Even if I struggle at times, giving my best effort will best help me succeed as I go forward." You may want to tailor this sample self-message to a sentence or two that fits better for you. The main thing to keep in mind is the value of centering yourself with a positive intention to keep you focused and less stressed out when you're doing schoolwork.

Using Realistic Thinking to Get Past Distorted Thoughts

Cognitive-behavioral therapy, which we introduced in chapter 4, is about challenging negative thinking by formulating more helpful, empowering thoughts. Following are some examples of overblown negative thoughts. These thoughts (technically termed "cognitive distortions") can create a whole range of self-doubts that march around in your mind like enemy soldiers, shooting holes in your positive intentions and standing in the way of your succeeding in school.

All-or-Nothing Thinking: You see things as either all good or bad. Many teens I work with, for example, feel that if they don't do everything near perfectly, they've failed. All-or-nothing thinking often includes the words "never" and "always." For example, you're struggling with a difficult writing assignment and you think, *I will never be able to get this done.* Another example of all-or-nothing thinking is *That test was so hard, I'm going to fail this class.*

Labeling: You rigidly stick a negative label on yourself. A frequent label that teens unfairly saddle themselves with when it comes to school is "lazy" or "stupid."

Shoulding: You have a list of rigid rules about how you and others should behave. Let's say you're frustrated about how long it's taking you to do a single math problem; an example of "shoulding" is the thought *This math problem shouldn't be so hard for me.* Sometimes teens, and even adults, think that beating themselves up with the word "should" makes them feel or look noble. The reality is that it leads to shame. And shame can surely lead you to feel down and sap your motivation to complete your schoolwork.

Negative Comparisons: You measure yourself against others and feel inferior, even though the comparison may not be realistic or helpful. For example, you have the thought *My classmates are way smarter than me.*

My teen clients say that building cognitive-behavioral therapy skills (such as through the following exercise) to battle distorted thoughts is a helpful complement to using mindfulness for managing school stress.

try this! Identifying Your School-Related Worries and Writing More Helpful Thoughts

Think about some of the school worries you have most often. Do tests, presentations, and homework demands trigger certain worries? What are some self-doubts you are having right now? On a piece of paper, create a table with two columns. In the first column, list some negative thoughts about school. Label the column "Worried Thoughts."

Just because your reacting brain leads you to doubt your abilities, that doesn't mean that you have to buy into these thoughts. Think about whether the thoughts you wrote down are true. Do they accurately reflect the situation and your abilities, or are they examples of distorted thinking? For each thought that you can identify as "all-or-nothing thinking," "labeling," "shoulding," or "negative comparison," write down a more helpful thought on the subject in the second column. For example, for the all-or-nothing thought *I will never understand this homework chapter*, you might write "Yeah, this chapter is tough, but I have made it through hard material before." If you wrote "I failed the science test, so I am stupid" (labeling), you might write "I didn't do well on this test, but that doesn't mean I'm stupid. I get better grades when I study more." If you wrote "I should have studied harder for the math test tomorrow" (shoulding), you might write "I'm willing to give it my best effort." If you wrote "Why did I get a C on that assignment when my partner got an A?" (negative comparison), you might write "I did my best, and I even improved from last time."

Afterward, reflect on whether writing more helpful thoughts increased your confidence in your ability to manage and meet your challenges. Does challenging your self-doubts with more helpful thoughts allow you to break free of them and be ready to do your best?

So far in this chapter we've covered some general mindfulness skills and mixed in some cognitive-behavioral therapy tools for addressing school struggles. This included mindful breathing, setting a positive intention, and working through school-related self-doubts.

Let's now turn to a big problem for teens that I will no longer put off: procrastination. Ugh! Now is the time to get off the procrastination train, because the next stop is worry wasteland.

Getting Out of the Procrastination Trap

Many teens express frustration to me about wrestling with procrastination. You most likely know what I'm talking about: putting off things like studying, homework, assignments, long-term projects, and, if you're a high-school senior, college applications.

Procrastination leads to a lot of worries, aggravation, and even all-nighters. You may even take out your procrastination-related irritability and angst on the people around you, such as your parents. As you have probably realized, this is not good for your relationships or your performance in school.

Why do so many teens procrastinate? Well, some procrastinate out of fear of not doing their schoolwork perfectly. Others feel overwhelmed and burned out from too many demands, so they rationalize that they "deserve" time to relax. Some teens share with me that they are "just not that into school" and would rather be doing anything else than schoolwork. Others tell me that they procrastinate because they are easily distractible. They find using their phones, watching TV, or playing video games to be immensely preferable to the drudgery of boring, perhaps even tedious, schoolwork.

Whatever the cause of your procrastination, it can creep up and overwhelm you. Remember that elephant you visualized in chapter 4? If you saw that elephant from the distance of a few football fields away, it would look very small. Now imagine that elephant is lumbering toward you while you're looking at your phone or other mobile device, not paying attention as time goes by. Once you realize the elephant is looming in front of you, it looks super big, doesn't it? This is what happens with procrastination—it makes you not see the demands that edge their way up until they have the ability to crush you.

Eddy's Story

Eddy, age seventeen, struggled with attention problems and worries about school when he first started to see me for counseling. One day, when discussing an overdue school project he was anxious about, he summed up his procrastination problem: "I just can't get my lazy butt to get anything done." He expressed having the best intentions to catch up in school but said, "When it comes down to it, I just distract myself with all the ways I can to avoid getting my work done."

Distractions play a big role in keeping teens like Eddie stuck in what I call the Procrastination Trap. Let's say that you're doing your homework and your cell phone buzzes or lights up with a text message. Are you going to check your phone or just keep doing your homework? I'm not a gambling man, but I'm guessing that you've been picking up that phone way too quickly and too often.

Given how distractions contribute to procrastinating, let's work on it—NOW.

In chapter 2, I introduced the acronym NOW to help you connect to three important parts of mindfulness: intention, attention, and attitude.

You can apply the NOW model for managing distractions by gaining awareness of what you are doing in the moment. An audio version of the following exercise is available at http://www.newharbinger.com/39812.

try this! Using NOW to Manage Distractions

As you sit down to do a school-related task (or imagine yourself doing so), take three mindful breaths and close your eyes. In this exercise, you'll (N) Notice distractions as competing for your attention, (O) Observe with curiosity how you feel pulled away by them, and (W) Willingly let them go in order to get back to what you need to do.

Notice: Notice yourself starting your homework. Reflect on your worries about getting through it and your urges to do something else, such as check out your phone or go online. Notice what you feel like. Are you freaking out about your schoolwork, angry that you have to do it, or seriously bored right now? Also notice any physical symptoms of worry (tightness in your stomach or chest, for example).

Observe (Open Up Your Curiosity): See and feel your intention to be in the moment and focusing on the task you need to complete.

Willingly Let Go: Willingly give yourself the gift of letting the distraction go. Gently remind yourself that you will feel better by completing your work.

Afterward, ask yourself how it felt to set an intention to manage distractions while doing (or imagining doing) your schoolwork. Can you see how gently gathering focus with mindfulness can help you stay more on target for getting your work done?

Practicing NOW can help you let go of urges to react to distractions. If you got sidetracked by a distraction during the preceding exercise, don't beat yourself up or say, "See, I can't do this." Setting intentions doesn't necessarily mean you'll always actually achieve your purpose, but they really do help you move in that direction. And, you will get better at managing distractions with practice. Let's wrap up this discussion of procrastination with a few more tips.

Try to clear away distractions. I know this is challenging, but try putting your phone or other mobile device out of reach. You may insist that you need to be able to go online to complete tasks for school, but the reality is that if you can voluntarily reduce distractions, you will less likely procrastinate and will be more productive with schoolwork.

Prioritize what task or part of a task is most important. When you have many different demands coming at you, everything seems important and can be overwhelming. This is why breaking big tasks down into parts makes the work feel less scary and helps get you moving. Also, by actively planning what to do, you are reconnecting with your intention to do it. If you have a book report due for school, this could mean selecting a topic, gathering sources, writing an outline, and committing to getting it done by a certain time.

Stay mindful of the benefits of completing the task to feel motivated. It may be hard to believe, but there's more benefit to getting assignments done than just getting them out of your hair. As you work, try to be mindful of the inner joy of learning and seeing your teachers and parents pleased with your efforts. Trust me, it's there to be found somewhere!

Homework, Tests, and Presentations

In closing this chapter, we will discuss using mindfulness with three more major sources of school worries. These are the challenges of homework, presentations, and exams.

Mindfully Managing Homework Stress

If you are like most teens, the word "homework" does not put you in a relaxed state of mind. The gentle, accepting spirit of mindfulness, however, can make homework a more pleasant and productive experience. Here is a list of tips that pulls together many of the mindfulness skills you have learned so far to make homework a more pleasurable experience.

- Take a few mindful breaths to feel relaxed.

- Check in with yourself and tune in to how you are feeling when starting your homework.

- Notice how your body feels and what is happening around you.

- Reflect on how you will feel better once you start on the task.

- Create a positive intention, and gently come back to it. Realize that it is common to have negative thoughts that can sap your motivation to do homework (e.g., *I hate doing this! I will never have to do it in real life* or *This is stupid and pointless*). Remind yourself that these are just thoughts; they don't have to stop you from doing your work. Let those negative thoughts pass by. Then empower yourself with a positive intention by saying something like, "Reminding myself to do my homework anyway, even when I don't want to do it, will help me feel better about both the assignment and myself."

- If you continue to feel frustrated or burned out, then take a mindfulness break. Think of a beautiful image from nature, such as a stream or a beach. Focus on the scene as if it were real, imagining everything you'd experience with your senses.

- Be willing to ask your teacher for help. To feel empowered to do this (many students are afraid to ask for help), gently remind yourself that the material is not supposed to come that easily to you. If that were the case, you'd be the teacher, not the student.

- Remember to take care of yourself by eating well, getting enough sleep, and valuing your homework efforts.

Now that you have learned some mindful tools for managing homework, let's get ready for those stressful tests.

Testing Out Mindfulness for Exams

Whether they are called quizzes, tests, or major exams, do you ever worry about taking them? My guess is that at times you really do—a lot! If you find yourself worried while cramming for a test, you may think, *I don't have the time to do this mindfulness stuff.* Trust me, though, that *really is* the time to do it—even briefly.

Mindfulness inserts calming energy into your worry-ridden mind and helps you better learn the material that you are studying. If you feel panicked by a thought such as *What if I fail?* just take a centering, mindful breath, pause, and remind yourself of all the class material that you do know. This can give you a shot of renewed confidence. Even if you continue to doubt yourself, reminding yourself that you can do better next time is reassuring as well.

While preparing for or even during a test, you can get out of worry wasteland by bringing yourself back to the present moment with mindful breaths, noticing "what is" around you, or just focusing on your senses. You can also do a mindfulness exercise like the following. Taking a brief pause to mindfully center yourself can calm your test anxiety and keep you from losing your focus.

try this! Getting Through a Test When You Feel Trapped by Worries

Take a few breaths. Feel the floor with your feet, and remind yourself that you are grounded. Notice feeling stuck and worried about the test. Briefly focus on your breath, and notice calming energy returning to you with each in-breath. With each out-breath, imagine that you are gently breathing out your test worries. Take your next breath and picture calming feelings and knowledge coming in. Visualize completing this test and congratulating yourself on your efforts and doing your best. If you feel stuck again, remember that you can take another breath at any time or even repeat the whole process.

Mindfully Preparing for Class Presentations

If the thought of doing a class presentation is really scary, mindfulness will help make it a less painful and more successful experience. In chapter 2, Sandy's story featured her mindfully reflecting on her thoughts and physical shakes about her upcoming presentation to manage her anxiety. Sandy shifted from worrying about standing in front of the class to wanting to share her knowledge with her peers.

If you approach your presentation efforts with beginner's mind (see chapter 2), prepare properly, and know your topic well, you may actually enjoy doing presentations. At the very least, the process will feel more tolerable. Keep the following tips in mind for making presentations a more pleasant experience.

- Prior to the time of your presentation, visualize where you will be giving your talk. During this

131

reflection, picture your worries drifting out the door from which you entered the room.

- Take several deep, long, relaxed breaths before you begin your presentation.

- Notice and gently resist any urges to rush. It is common for worried teens to speed through a presentation to get it over with, but rushing it can heighten your anxiety.

- To avoid rushing, share your information in a spirit of curiosity, as though you were just learning about it yourself. This will help your audience focus more on your topic instead of how you are presenting it. If worries come your way, gently take a breath and reconnect to a calmer state.

- Even though your peers probably have no choice but to listen to you, try to have appreciation for their attention. You may want to begin your presentation by thanking your peers for their attention. This can help you feel more confident and ease your worries.

This All Sounds Good, but "What If?"

If I had a dollar for every "what if" my teen clients share about their school worries, I'd be rich! "What ifs" can pop up in your mind at any moment, even when you're being mindful, and can really hobble your school performance unless you learn to manage them.

In chapter 1, we discussed Wes and his "What ifs." If you recall, he initially struggled with "What ifs" about failing an exam, and his continuing "What if" worries had him catastrophizing that he'd end up living on the street.

Here is how Wes dealt with his upsetting "What ifs": He first took a few deep breaths to re-center himself. He then noticed his "What ifs" in a different way, from an outsider's perspective, without reacting to them. He also looked around at his surroundings and noticed "what is" around him. After taking a few more mindful breaths to slow down his racing mind, Wes used a cognitive-behavioral strategy to challenge some of his "What if" thoughts. He learned to say to himself, *What's the worst thing that can happen?* each time he got worried about "What ifs."

Mindfully and calmly considering the worst-case scenario—asking yourself *What's the worst that can happen?*—will help you move beyond your worries. This is because the worst-case situation is usually not as bad as you worry that it will be. Here are some examples of how to talk back to your "What ifs."

What if?	What's the Worst That Can Happen?
What if I fail this test?	I will work harder and do better next time.
What if I can't get this homework done?	I'll try to complete it before class.
What if I fail the class?	I will take it in summer school or next year.
What if I can't get into a good college?	I will find one I still like that I can get into.

Give it a try for yourself in the following exercise.

try this! Getting to the Bottom of Your "What Ifs"

Reflect on some of your own troublesome "What ifs." Write them on a piece of paper. Now challenge yourself to answer those questions in a way that shows that the worst-case scenario is very unlikely or not a total disaster from which you can't recover.

As a variation of this challenge, turn each "What if?" into "So what if?" For example, if you worry, *What if I can't get my homework done?* you might challenge that worry with *So what if I can't get my home-work done?* By adding "so" before "What if," you will change the worry into a way to explore how to solve the problem and not just worry about it. As you can see, asking "So what if?" has the same empower-ing, positive impact as asking "What's the worst that can happen?" Try them both out if you are getting caught up in "What ifs," and pick the one you feel most comfortable with to use.

In this chapter, you learned about the causes of worries about school and how to manage your school-related worries with mindfulness. You also learned some cognitive-behavioral strategies to challenge your self-doubts and refocus on your strengths for success in school. Moving forward, you can manage any tendencies to procrastinate using the acronym NOW. Mindfulness will also keep you in a positive state of mind for handling the challenges of homework, tests, and pre-sentations. Here is what teens like you had to say about using mindfulness to manage school-related stress.

Teens in Their Own Words

"Other kids had no idea how freaked out I was on the morning bus going to school. But using mindfulness made me feel less worried about it. I can't say I do mindful exercises all the time, but it just helps to know it is there to help me relax if I need it." —Austin, age thirteen

"I'm not gonna lie. I first thought mindfulness was really dumb. But seriously, now, before I take a test, I think of a calm image like the stream in my backyard or a beach I went to, using all my senses to imagine what it would be like to be there, and I really calm down fast." —Trent, age fourteen

"It totally helps me chill out. I take some deep breaths before Spanish class, and now I can finally put up with my seriously boring teacher." —Dana, age fifteen

"My grades actually went up this year, and I really think it was the mindfulness stuff that stopped me from so much worrying about school and helped me do better in it." —Carlos, age seventeen

Now that you have practiced mindfulness to cope with school pressures, in the next chapter you'll learn to manage socially-related worries that come with being a teen.

chapter 7

managing social worries with mindfulness

How many times do you smile while crying on the inside?

—*Anonymous*

You likely want to feel as if you belong and fit in with your peers. It's a great feeling to connect with others and know that they care about you. Teens often open up to me about this strong need for joining with others. Feeling accepted and understood by friends helps get you through rough times.

The desire to feel accepted and maintain friendships, however, can also be the source of painful feelings and worries. The strong urge to belong can lead to pressure to be seen positively by your peers. You probably want to be viewed as popular, cool, and accepted—to look as though you have it totally together. Otherwise, you may worry, other kids could judge you harshly. And they might not do it to your face; they might gossip about you on social media. Thus, the fear of looking awkward, "messing up," being put down, not being liked, or even being abandoned can really feel overwhelming. And what about dating and relationships? Those things are likely even more stressful! How do you deal with all the worries this can cause?

In this chapter, we will look at the causes of social worries. Then you'll learn mindfulness skills to help you manage social pressures and tensions in your friendships. We'll talk about how being mindful can lead to better communication both in person and through electronic devices. Finally, we'll touch upon the topic of dating relationships.

First, let's look at why making and keeping close social connections is so important for teens.

Deeper Feelings Deepen Your Friendships

As a teen, you have matured a lot and moved well beyond the casual, free-flowing friendships of past elementary school years. You are also drifting away from your family members, to some degree. Nowadays, sharing time with or communicating with friends likely often feels more comfortable than hanging out with your parents. In general, relationships have become more complex for you. Your maturing brain has stronger preferences for who you can best relate to and connect with.

I appreciate the stories teens share with me that show how much their friends mean to them. Sometimes the stories are funny ones. I also hear many heartfelt accounts of teens supporting each other through the struggles of growing up. Following are some specific reasons you may be led to form strong friendship bonds:

- You are drawn to peers who share your interests and views on life. (Some teens, though, "try on" new identities, making friends who may have very dissimilar interests.)

- You value friendships that are close and tightly knit. You may even turn to friends instead of family members for support when you feel worried or upset.

- Trust and loyalty mean a lot to you. You want your friends to support you in stressful times, and they want to feel that you are there for them too.

- You like the sense of independence that comes from having a circle of friends.

- Friends help you develop a personal style that is all your own (because what teenager wants to talk, dress, and behave just like his or her parents?) but not too different from your peers. Feeling similar to your peers keeps you feeling close to and accepted by them.

- You really feel a need for privacy about intimate feelings you have toward others, which includes crushes and relationships that you are involved in. You want friends who can keep secrets.

Social Strain Leads to Emotional Pain

Social relationships with your fellow teens can be very satisfying, but they are not all sunshine and rainbows. Teens often face disappointment or emotional pain in social situations such as those involving:

Having spoken or unspoken feelings of competitiveness and jealousy

Having text or verbal arguments

Being ignored

Listening to or passing on rumors

Feeling bullied or bullying others

These are huge sources of stress for teens. Social media, which we will discuss soon, can really worsen conflicts. The "news" of peer problems and conflicts can, for better or worse, spread like wildfire and be very emotionally hurtful. Misunderstandings that get whispered down the lane can result in teens suddenly feeling betrayed or even abandoned by their friends.

Teens tell me that social worries, such as looking awkward, being overlooked, or being rejected, are scary because their relationships feel so crucial and valuable. I occasionally hear stories of teens feeling humiliated and shamed by peers and even friends as a result of tasteless teasing, nasty lies, and controversial comments. Just anticipating the possibility of being bullied, teased, or simply talked about understandably sends many teens into worry wasteland. Yet most don't want to show it. They want to look confident and unconcerned, because admitting or even appearing to have social anxiety may, on its own, attract negative attention. Teens tell me that they attempt to hide their worries about their social lives by acting as if everything is "fine."

Teens sometimes admit to me that appearing happy on the outside sharply contrasts with their social insecurities. They tell others that they're feeling "fine" when in fact they feel quite different. Rather than "good" or "great," sometimes "fine" really means FINE:

(F) Foolish, Frustrated, or Freaked out

(I) Insecure, Insignificant, or Invisible

(N) Nervous, Neglected, or Not Enough

(E) Embarrassed, Emotional, or Empty

The point is that most teens try to keep their social worries hidden from their peers and others. But trust me, every teen gets worked up over fears of not fitting in and of feeling rejected.

You may know a few teens who give off that vibe of, "I never worry about what other people think of me." Don't believe it. The reality is that we all struggle with some level of insecurities about our connections with others.

I am pleased to share that some of my most powerful counseling experiences have been with those few teens and adults who felt really misunderstood because everyone else mistakenly thought their lives were "perfect." Even though some of these teens may appear to have won the genetic lottery for being physically attractive, athletic, and really smart, they often share hidden worries and fears about being good enough, too.

Teens who seemingly have it all together, and even who may be super popular, confide in me that that they feel a crazy amount of pressure to keep being seen that way. These "flawless teens" describe pressures to live up to their perfect image. They, like everyone else, have worries, and learn that it is actually

141

healthier to acknowledge the inner struggles that come with being FINE.

Here is what some teens had to say about their fears of not appearing socially secure.

Teens in Their Own Words

"I feel like I'm just there but I don't fit in." —Derek, age thirteen

"When I see a group of people laughing, I automatically first think they are laughing about me." —Maria, age fourteen

"It just seems like everybody in my grade hangs out with the upper- and lower-classmen and people from different schools, and I barely know people in my grade." —Colin, age fifteen

"It is so unfair that I am labeled as a slut just because I kissed him." —Becky, age fifteen

"I kind of keep my head tilted down and make myself unapproachable. I feel like if I try to talk to someone, they will just brush me off, especially if it is a girl." —Jake, age sixteen

"I often worry that people think I'm strange and not worth getting to know." —Fernando, age nineteen

"I Have to Fix Myself If I Want to Fit In"

Most teens, at one time or another, act in a certain way in order to fit in, even if it goes against how they really feel or what they feel like doing.

Sergio's Story

Sergio, age sixteen, was very athletic and popular. But after learning that his girlfriend had cheated on him with a football player from a rival school, he felt devastated. He was afraid to let his friends know how upset he was, feeling that he had to act "tough" to keep their respect. When he did confide in a friend, that friend trash-talked the girl, not understanding that Sergio still had feelings for her. In my counseling practice, guiding Sergio through some mindfulness exercises and "allowing" him to accept the feelings he had for his now ex-girlfriend helped Sergio move beyond his feelings of loss, embarrassment, and shame.

Peer pressure, whether it's real or imagined, can be very strong. You may worry, like Britany, that people will judge you simply on who you hang out with and whether *they* fit in.

Britany's Story

Britany and Vanessa had a strong friendship. Vanessa, feeling safe in this friendship, began to confide about her transgender issues to Britany. The ever-present teenage need to fit in caused Britany to worry what her other friends would think about her friendship with Vanessa if word got out about Vanessa's transgender concerns. As an open-minded and independent teen, she felt ashamed for having these worries, so she started to beat herself up for her anxiety.

In counseling, I encouraged Britany to explore her worries without judgment. It helped her move beyond the concerns of what others might think. Feeling empowered to support her friend, Britany encouraged Vanessa to see the school counselor, who referred Vanessa to a therapist specializing in transgender issues. Britany felt comfort in knowing that her good friend was getting professional support.

Peering in at Peer Pressure

Peer pressure can lead you to do things that are contrary to your real interests or goals. For some teens, giving in to peer pressure may be something like hanging out talking or texting because it's what your friends want to do, even though you'd rather get started on homework. Or, maybe a sweet talking friend coaxed you to sign up for an activity or sport that you really are just not into doing. Another scenario of getting pulled in by a friend could be following his lead to skip an assignment or a class. Teens also, at times, tell me how they experience peer pressure to experiment with drugs and alcohol.

try this! Mindfully Reflecting on Peer Pressure

Take a few deep breaths to help clear your mind. When you're ready, reflect on times in your life when you have faced pressure from peers to act a certain way or make certain decisions. How have you positively influenced or negatively impacted your peers by perhaps pressuring them to make certain choices? Consider how peer pressure has helped you at times. Then think about the opposite: What, if any, peer-pressure situations led to a regrettable decision or an unpleasant outcome?

Afterward, feel gratitude for being open to learning and growing from these experiences.

Caring vs. Worrying with Friends

Let's talk now about a different source of social worries. Friends often worry about one another. If you have a friend who's in an unhealthy relationship, not trying hard enough in school, or making bad decisions, it can be painful to watch. Maybe you have given this friend good advice and he or she hasn't listened, so all you can do now is worry. Or maybe you're worried over something upsetting your friend told you is going on in his or her life, such as conflicts with family members, concerns about sexual experiences, problems with a teacher, being dumped by someone, using drugs, or engaging in self-harming behaviors such as cutting.

It is easy to feel pulled deeply into your friends' problems, but your taking on their worries will not help them. In fact, overly worrying and burdening yourself with friends' problems will just drain you of valuable caring energy.

Gary's Story

Gary, a high school junior, had a very close group of friends. Several were in many of the same classes, others he saw regularly on his baseball team, and several of his friends were female classmates. Gary's friends really appreciated that he was a good listener. They sensed that he truly cared about them.

Gary, in turn, felt a sense of pride that he could be there for all of his friends. This included a very anxious female classmate, Charlene. Charlene would share her concerns with him, and he would listen and occasionally give advice. He began to feel very close to her and developed a crush. When she began to share with him about cutting herself in response to being rejected by a mutual male friend of theirs, Gary started to feel flooded with anxiety. He began having a difficult time getting to sleep, became more irritable, and started to slip in his school performance.

In time, it became even harder for Gary to keep himself together, especially when his academic demands further intensified along with his sports obligations. These time-crunching stresses piled on top of his worries about Charlene's problems. Feeling overwhelmed, Gary lashed out at home, especially toward his mother. (Fortunately, Gary's mom could sense what was going on and didn't take it personally. Sensing his mother's non-judgmental attitude, Gary then opened up to her and sorted out his feelings, realizing in the end that being a friend to Charlene didn't have to mean trying to solve all of her problems).

In the last chapter, we discussed the difference between caring about your schoolwork and worrying about it. The same mindfulness principle of setting a caring intention can be applied to your friendships. Mindfulness can help you be tuned in and present when it comes to balancing being supportive with your friends without feeling burdened by their struggles. Drawing upon mindfulness will give you that pause to stay calm and centered to listen with compassion, and, if your friends desire, to help guide them to solve their problems.

try this! Carrying vs. Worrying About Your Friends' Problems

Imagine listening to one of your friend's problems. Picture these problems coming toward you, drifting around you, and moving past you.

While doing this, send your friend caring energy and empathy. Notice the conversation coming to a close, and focus on the positive feelings of supporting your friend while letting his or her problems stay behind you and drift away. Notice how it feels to help your friend while maintaining healthy, caring boundaries in the process.

Friendships go through ups and downs for various reasons. For example, friends may sometimes take each other for granted or feel bored with each other. Or, if you or a friend are caught up in worries, you may feel disconnected and drift away from each other. Minor disagreements can also take a toll and create distance between friends. Teens have also sadly shared with me about bigger disagreements or fall-outs. Some regret the ending of friendships that meant a lot to them and that they wish still existed. In a similar way that houses, roads, and even your computer or phone need to be maintained and taken care of, so do your friendships for them to last. Mindfully maintaining your friendships will help keep worries about the health of your friendships away.

Following is a great way to nourish those you care about by sending them positive energy in your own mind. It may sound weird, but it works.

try this! Embracing Love and Kindness

Take a few breaths. As you breathe in and out, picture the faces of your friends. Let the caring and value you see in your friends arise before your mind's eye (draw from your experiences and feelings about them to enhance the mental image). Reflect on their faces with gratitude as you appreciate what each of them brings to you and teaches you. Feel the positive energy you gain from having them as your friends. Now

147

close your eyes and take a few mindful breaths and imagine sending a wave of caring, supportive energy to your friends. Feel your heart beat with joy and gratitude for the gift of your friendships.

Afterward, do you feel as if there's more caring energy in your heart to help your friendships thrive and survive? How might tuning in to the value of your friendships help you value yourself?

Having a caring intention is important in friendships. At the same time, caring only goes so far unless you have effective communication with your friends. We all know how saying or hearing the wrong thing can really strain relationships. So let's now build on the intention for mindful communication by discussing what it consists of.

The Gift of Mindful Communication

Your connections with others will be more meaningful as you engage in mindful conversations. Being mindful when you have conversations with your peers, and others, means being as present as you can when you communicate. The main elements for mindful communication are listening closely without judgment, speaking clearly, and being honest and truthful. Let's start with mindful listening—a challenge for all of us.

Mindful Listening

How great would you feel if your friends listened to you as if you were a celebrity that they admired and respected? You would likely treasure that experience. In contrast, have you ever caught yourself during a conversation, rather than listening to what the other person is saying, being more concerned with what you were going to say next? How about that "ouch feeling" when the other person realized that you had been spacing out and not really listening? Rest assured that this happens to many of my teen clients and to me, too.

try this! Practicing Mindful Listening

You can arrange to do this exercise with a particular friend, practice it spontaneously during a conversation with him or her, or just imagine that you're having a conversation with this person.

Take a few breaths and reflect on your intention to really listen. Next, listen attentively without judgment. Maintain good eye contact without interrupting your friend. When he or she pauses for you to respond, remember that your tone and body language count. Leaning in slightly without slouching; being kind in your tone; maintaining solid, supportive eye contact; and saying "mm-hmm" or nodding to show agreement can go a long way in being a mindful listener. This caring, mindful awareness will help you better listen to your friend's words. Notice how mindful listening feels and whether your friend seems to appreciate it.

Afterward, reflect on whether listening mindfully left you feeling more connected. Can you see how mindful listening helps you more accurately understand others and communicates that you care?

Speaking Mindfully

Once you've got mindful listening down, it is time to focus on speaking mindfully. Mindful speaking is all about being aware of how the feelings and thoughts you express impact others and reflect upon you. I call this having a "Ready, Set, Go" intention instead of falling into the trap of speaking impulsively.

By being aware of how you express your thoughts and feelings, you will less likely rush in to interrupt and say what you don't really mean or prattle on. Keep in mind that in our fast-paced, distracted world, speaking mindfully can be challenging. Interrupting or rambling is something everyone does—but if we bring mindful attention to our speaking, it happens less often. And when it does happen, we can catch ourselves and adjust, bringing our words back to mindful speech.

try this! Giving Mindful Speaking a Go

As with the mindful listening exercise, you can arrange to do this with a particular friend, practice it spontaneously during a conversation with him or her, or just do it in your imagination.

Take a few breaths, and reflect on your intention to really listen. When it is your time to respond to what your friend has said, take a few deep, calming breaths as you gently notice, without judgment, how you are thinking and feeling. Express yourself openly (within reason), and if there is conflict, try to avoid reacting by blaming (shifting the conflict entirely onto your friend), criticizing (throwing out negative comments that shut down your friend from speaking), or using judgmental words (expressing that your friend is below you). Notice how mindful speaking works for you and how your friend seems to respond.

We have so far addressed ways to understand, build, and strengthen friendships in a proactive manner. But what about when you and your friends find yourself up Conflict Creek without a paddle? Let's now turn to managing peer conflicts with mindfulness.

When Conflicts Arise

Most teens don't like conflict, even those who claim to thrive on drama. Conflicts with peers can create big-time anxiety. But conflict, whether spoken or unspoken, is inevitable. When it happens, you may worry about how big it will get, how long it will last, how widely it will spread, and potential gossip that can arise from it.

Check out the example of conflict in Ruth's story, which illustrates when "just joking" feels hurtful.

Ruth's Story

Ruth was a freshman in high school. One day she was talking to two friends she had made that year, Teresa and Maya.

The conversation was light-hearted, and all three girls were laughing. Then Ruth mentioned her crush, Brendan. Teresa laughingly said that Ruth was waaay out of his league. Teresa took it further by saying that Ruth and Brendan could never look like a cute couple. When Ruth, understandably now flustered, briefly looked away, Teresa realized the need for damage control and said, "Hey, just joking—you'd probably be good together."

Later in the day, after incessantly replaying Teresa's initial comment in her mind, Ruth saw Maya in the hallway and said: "Hey, did you see how Teresa—Miss 'I'm a hot cheerleader!'—was treating me like crap? I really like Brendan, and she was so mean and clueless. How could she say that to me? She always has to put everyone else down to feel good about herself. I just can't stand her."

Fortunately, Ruth, at Maya's urging, later told Teresa that she felt hurt by her negative comments about being out of Brendan's league. Teresa at first downplayed her comment to Ruth, reminding her that at the time she had said, "just joking." Seeing how hurt Ruth still felt, however, Teresa then owned up to her mistake and offered a heartfelt apology, and the two moved past this conflict.

Working through conflicts, as you probably know, is much healthier than bottling them and stewing over them. Ruth, who was my client in counseling, had used the NOW model to help her prepare to discuss her concerns with Teresa. NOW was first discussed in chapter 2 to help you practice mindful acceptance and letting go of painful feelings. Let's revisit NOW to mindfully let go of conflicts with peers.

try this! Letting Go of a Peer Conflict Using NOW

Take three centering, calming breaths. Think about the types of conflicts you have with friends that trigger upsetting feelings for you.

- **(N) Notice:** Reflect on a past conflict with a friend, or imagine having a conflict, and notice how you are feeling and what is upsetting you.

- **(O) Observe (Open Up Your Curiosity):** Observe the interaction and conflict by imagining you are looking down on the scene from above. Picture yourself floating on the ceiling, looking down at both you and your friend. If the conflict occurred through text messages or social media, notice your thoughts and feelings about that as well. Observe your reactions about the conflict without judgment.

- **(W) Willingly Let Go:** Release the conflict by giving yourself a little coaching, telling yourself that you will just feel worse if you continue to dwell on or magnify it. Reflect on your strength to rise above this conflict as a tolerant, forgiving friend.

Afterward, consider the extent to which moving to NOW gave you emotional space to pause and slow down your racing mind and realize that you didn't have to react out of anger or fear.

Can you see how the next time that you may have a conflict or argument with a friend, mindfully practicing NOW can help you let go of the conflict? Keep this exercise in mind the next time an upsetting situation with a friend arises.

Let's now focus on the world of digital communication, including texting and social media, since this is sometimes where conflicts start or can spread.

Staying Afloat in the Strong Currents of Social Media

Social media offers teens amazing opportunities to connect with friends and others. It is fun and exciting to see what is happening online, make connections, and have people respond to your posts as well as respond to theirs. What teen doesn't like getting "liked"?

At the same time, social media can springboard teens into worry wasteland. Seeing posts from friends and other peers can trigger both positive and negative thoughts and feelings. For example, you may feel happy for a friend who posted an achievement she was proud of but also feel left out when seeing pictures of her at a party you wish you had been invited to.

Earlier we discussed using healthy intentions to navigate between caring and worrying about your friends. The mindfulness skill of setting helpful intentions to manage your reactions and feelings to social situations is also valuable whenever you go online. A positive intention could help, for example, if you see your best friend's recent ex posting a picture of himself with a new girlfriend (or boyfriend) and you know that it might devastate your friend. Another upsetting situation might be seeing the way that one of your friends is virtually ignored on social media. Or maybe someone you really don't get along with or have a hard time trusting is now edging into your social group, and you're worried about the effect that might have on your circle of friends.

try this! Managing Social Media with Self-Valuing Intentions

Take a few deep breaths, and have a mindful spirit of gentle curiosity as you log in to your favorite social media site. Stay tuned in to what you are thinking and feeling. Note how you are feeling physically (Are you tense, or are you loose and relaxed?) and emotionally (Are you eager, insecure, worried, calm, valued, or deflated?). If worries come up—about a status you posted that no one's liked, or a party someone invited everyone in your clique to except you—meet them in a mindful way; meet them in the NOW. That is, Notice, Observe, and be Willing to let them go. Be aware of your value as a person, and feel pride about the joy you bring to others in your life. Social media is no doubt a way to expand your social experiences. Just keep in mind how it can positively enrich you on one hand and how it can negatively impact you on the other. Repeat to yourself: "Social media is just one part of my being a socially connected person. It does not define my value as a person."

Afterward, reflect on whether holding a self-valuing intention of your social media experience felt more affirming and healthy than mindlessly being sucked into it. Did having a more mindful approach to social media help you avoid impulsively posting something or responding in a way you would likely have later regretted?

In much the same way, being mindfully aware when you text offers a valuable gift of "quality control" to ensure you write what you mean and mean what you write.

try this! Mindful Texting

Reflect on having a "Ready, Set, Go!" intention, as we discussed earlier, and consider not rushing your text messaging. Imagine yourself receiving a text message, or try this the next time you receive one

Center yourself with a few mindful breaths to create a healthy, reflective pause (teens tell me a count to ten is helpful) to notice your surroundings with your senses, or focus on a pleasant image to give you a pause to respond meaningfully. Use this mindful pause to text back thoughtfully as opposed to impulsively.

Afterward, reflect on whether this exercise was easy or challenging. Did you feel less pressure than usual to respond too quickly? Can you think of a downside to being more measured before you respond to text messages?

Let's spend the last part of this chapter addressing worries from the world of teen intimacy. Even if you are not currently in a relationship, it's worthwhile to do some mindful self-exploration about what intimacy means to you in general.

Mindfulness for Dating and Intimate Relationships

As a teen, being in a healthy relationship is a wonderful joy to have in your life. You can feel safe, valued, and fulfilled by having someone special in your life. Mindfulness gives teens tools for awareness, honesty, and positive intention that support and strengthen their relationships. If you use the previously discussed tips for mindful listening and speaking in your intimate relationships, they will be infused with a lot of healthy, caring energy.

Ironically, our closest relationships also tend to present us with the biggest challenges in our lives. This is especially the case for teens, as you are going through so many emotional and physical changes and life transitions at the same time. Given all these pressures and worries, teen relationships are often like roller coasters with lots of rapid ups and downs. In romantic relationships, teens make themselves vulnerable to others with whom they feel that special connection. Teens' fear of being hurt while feeling vulnerable in intimate relationships are, therefore, very understandable.

As a teen in an intimate relationship, the worrying part of your brain likely gets filled with insecurities and fears, and the result can be flipping your lid, as we discussed in chapter 1. Teens tell me, for example, that if their boyfriend or girlfriend does not quickly respond to a text message it may trigger insecurity. This may be fueled by their inner "shoulding": *She or he should have responded by now if he or she really cared.*

We discussed the awesome power of acceptance in chapter 4. Acceptance in the context of relationships is about understanding each other's strengths and struggles. Realizing that it is okay to not be perfect and that every relationship takes work can help put your worries to rest.

Following are signs of healthy acceptance in teen relationships:

- Recognizing that neither you nor your partner will be happy all the time

- Being willing to grow from misunderstandings

- Realizing that accepting challenges never means embracing being mistreated or hurt

Practice managing upsetting feelings about your relationship in the following exercise.

try this! Managing Upsetting Feelings in Your Relationship

Take a few calming breaths. Picture yourself in a heated moment with your boyfriend or girlfriend. Reflect on how you feel hurt and/ or angry. Now imagine observing these thoughts and emotions and thoughts without getting caught up in them. By noticing these feelings without judging them, you can regain a sense of your emotional balance. Maybe you see ways your girlfriend or boyfriend behaved less than trustfully—and ways you reacted less than respectfully to his or her behavior. Or vice versa: maybe it was you who didn't trust your partner, and your partner reacted too harshly. Seeing all this—and just seeing it, without judging it—allows you to think about how your instinctive reactions compare to how you would *like* to respond. Mindfulness in loving relationships helps you notice your thoughts and feelings without overreacting. This can help minimize conflicts, giving you less to worry about.

Afterward, can you see how mindfulness helps you slow down your emotions to experience your relationship in a calmer way? Do you think that rehearsing how to handle conflicts in your relationship will be useful?

Your intimate relationships will function more smoothly when you employ mindfulness to help you maintain respect and trust.

Following are signs of respect in teen relationships:

- Treating the other person as a friend

- Being proud of who you each are as individuals and as a couple

- Speaking and listening to the other person in a caring, emotionally safe way

Following are signs of trust in teen relationships:

- Having respect when communicating with the other person (whether face to face or through text or instant messaging)

- Being okay with each of you spending time alone

- Being able to spend time with friends outside of your relationship

- Not jumping to conclusions about the other person's behavior when you feel misgivings

When a Relationship No Longer Meets Your Needs

Teens often tell me they're in an intimate relationship that is no longer satisfying. Yet many worry about how it would hurt their boyfriend's or girlfriend's feelings to end the relationship. Others describe feeling anxious about being the center of gossipy attention, especially if the rumor mill churns out unfavorable or unsavory stories about the breakup. Even though breakups can be upsetting, teens have confided in me that being free of the struggles of a relationship that was not satisfying to them also brought them a strong sense of relief.

The way you think about ending a relationship can really help you manage your worries. As discussed in chapter 1, approaching your concerns by caring versus worrying can keep you out of worry wasteland. It also really helps if you see all relationships as learning experiences. The less you see a breakup as a flop or a failure, the more you can see it as an opportunity to be grateful for your openness to connecting with someone you valued in a deep, special way. Relationships that end can help you understand yourself better too—for example, they can help you determine the degree to which you value together versus alone time or the level of independence versus sense of commitment that feels manageable to you.

If you find yourself wanting to move out of your relationship, it is important that you be open, honest, and respectful in doing so. The old standby line "I just need space," especially if you have an attraction to someone else, can feel very misleading to the person you want to end the relationship with. And breaking up by suddenly not responding to someone's text messages or by texting that person "I can't see you anymore" is even more cruel. Give yourself time to mindfully reflect on the relationship you are leaving, noting what worked well and what didn't, and take some time before moving on. Whether the end of the relationship is mutual or not, taking the high road and keeping any possible negative feelings under control is the way to go.

In this chapter, you learned about the causes and triggers of worries in social connections, friendships, and intimate relationships.

You practiced mindfulness for navigating worries and conflicts with peers. We discussed social media as another source of worries and as an opportunity for you to use mindfulness to manage them. You also learned the value of practicing mindfulness for better communication. We addressed the value of mindfulness for managing the worries and emotionally intense challenges that can occur in teen dating relationships.

Here is what some teens had to say about how mindfulness helped them with social worries:

Teens in Their Own Words

"Ugh! Sometimes it just gets so scary worrying what other people think of me. By learning to notice people around me in a curious but less judgmental way, with a mindful attitude, I'm not just focusing on my worries like I used to."
—Bianca, age fourteen

"Mindfulness helped me see that getting worried about social situations doesn't mean I'm messed up. Doing the breathing or visualizing cool things or noticing what is going on around me helps me get out of my head, even if I still feel a little jittery. This stops my anxiety from taking over and making me just want to stay home instead of hanging out with friends."
—Tyler, age fifteen

"I feel like mindfulness gives me the confidence to believe in myself more in social situations. The nonjudgmental stuff that goes with mindfulness takes the pressure off me feeling like I have to measure up to others all the time."
—Lyla, age seventeen

In the next chapter, we will discuss another special relationship that tends to be stressful for teens—your relationship with your body, known as body image.

chapter 8

mindfulness for a positive body image

… And I said to my body softly, "I want to be your friend." It took a long breath. And replied, "I have been waiting my whole life for this."

—Nayyirah Waheed

"Body image" refers to how you view and feel about your physical self and how you believe others view your appearance. If you often get caught up in worries about your appearance, then learning to manage these upsetting feelings can really help you feel better.

Have you ever wondered why some of your less attractive peers don't seem especially concerned about the way they look? And why is it that, on the other hand, some really attractive people worry about the tiniest details? It's because, when it comes to your body image, how you think about and view your appearance plays a huge role. Flawed thinking, not a flawed body, is at the core of your body-image concerns. In this chapter, we will discuss some specific triggers of body-image anxiety and have you use your mindfulness skills to practice defusing these potential threats to your self-esteem. Then I'll share some tips for maintaining a healthy, positive body image.

Teens tell me that—although they generally keep this fact to themselves—they find it difficult to have a positive body image. They may like the way certain parts of their bodies look but dislike the way other parts look. Many teens worry that if they're not attractive enough, their acceptance, popularity, and romantic prospects will be limited. If the mirror doesn't show them exactly what they want to see (or what they think others want to see), they may feel frustration and even self-hatred. Some teens have told me that they worry that if they don't look good enough, they may be ignored by or even rejected from desired peer groups. That is some serious body-image pressure to contend with!

Teen Body Image: A Struggle for Both Genders

Teenage girls feel considerable pressure to be thin and look pretty in order to be popular. Teen guys feel similar pressure to be popular by enhancing their appearance, which often leads to efforts to look muscular or physically strong.

Some teen girls tell me they need to be sought after by good-looking guys in order to feel attractive. Because they want to fit those guys' "type," they feel pressure to eat less, wear a lot of makeup, and have perfect-looking hair. Some girls also mention feeling pressure to be friends with popular girls to give the impression that they are popular as well.

Guys similarly confide to me that they seek out the attention of the "hot girls" to try to validate their own attractiveness. They say they are not "supposed" to express body-image worries because, if they do, they will appear weak. Yet many have told me they worry about taking off their shirts in the locker room or at the beach for fear of their upper bodies looking too small or thin, or too big, or flabby.

Now that you have explored the general concept of body image, let's discuss those four specific concerns over which teens often struggle with their appearance.

Four Body-Image Triggers of Your Reactive Brain

Teens express to me these common triggers for worries about their bodies: physical changes due to puberty, comparing themselves negatively to their peers, images of perfection in the media (especially social media), and family dynamics.

Noticing How Puberty Is Changing Your Body

When you were younger, did you learn about all the physical changes that would take place during puberty? Even if you know what to expect, puberty can be quite shocking once you start to go through it. You may think: *Whoa! Is this really happening to my body?* People talk about kids "hitting puberty," but some days you may feel it's the other way around, more as though puberty is hitting you!

As you well know, puberty usually begins at age nine to ten for girls and around age twelve for boys. Thus even before they're teenagers, boys' and girls' bodies start to go through sudden, drastic transformations. Some girls gain extra fat, which may or may not be temporary, right before a growth spurt. Others grow tall and slim. Girls start to have menstrual periods, begin growing breasts, and become taller than boys in their grade.

Boys develop deeper voices, and their bodies fill out, as they grow taller too. They start having tenderness and breast-tissue enlargement behind their nipples. They also start to get erections, which can occur at random, causing discomfort and embarrassment.

Both boys and girls may develop acne not only on their faces but also on other parts of their bodies. They begin to have adult body odor, which, while only natural, can feel very embarrassing before they learn to manage it.

All this may take several years, but each change may seem to occur suddenly. And, at any given point, there's bound to be something about your physical appearance that makes you feel insecure. Whenever you look in the mirror, you may obsess about something that seems weird, goofy, or ugly. You may wish you had a taller, thinner, or curvier body, clearer skin, straighter or curlier hair, or a differently shaped or sized nose. Or you may simply think *Yikes!* It can be easy to get stuck in worry wasteland with concerns about what people will think and how they'll respond to your appearance.

Teens in Their Own Words

"My chest gets sore. The doctor said this is normal, but I am afraid to take off my T-shirt at the beach because my friends tell me I have 'man boobs.' I keep this to myself and hope no one will look at me or say anything." —Kareem, age fourteen

"I gained weight this year and I feel fat. Now I'm freaking out that I won't have a thigh gap in my bikini at the beach." —Melony, age fourteen

"I feel self-conscious about my acne, and that makes me want to avoid looking at people." —Blake, age sixteen

"I am still flat-chested, and it really bothers me." —Linette, age seventeen

"I hate how all the guys just think I am hot and stare at my chest. I feel pressure to live up to always having to look good, yet no one takes my intelligence seriously." —Monica, age eighteen

Although mindfulness won't influence how puberty changes your body during your teen years, I can offer you the next best thing: learning how to feel more at peace with your body during this period of rapid physical change. Teens tell me the following sort of mindfulness exercise helps them a lot.

try this! **Making Peace with Your Changing Body**

Take a deep breath. As you breathe in, tell yourself silently, *I feel accepting of my changing body.* As you breathe out, say, *My love for my changing body is constant.* Do this three times.

Now hug yourself with self-compassion and set an intention to feel accepting of your body's changes.

Breathe in with affirming gratitude for being able to think about your body in a less judgmental way.

Afterward, consider how it felt to view your body's changes in a more mindfully accepting way. Can you see how acceptance of your bodily changes can help you feel freer to have a more positive body image?

Now that we have explored understanding your puberty-related changes and introduced a mindful way to relate to them, let's consider how you may worry when comparing yourself to your peers.

Comparing Yourself Negatively to Your Peers

You likely want to feel that you look good compared to those around you. As we discussed in chapter 7, it is easy to feel socially self-conscious when walking through the hallways in school. I feel empathy for teens who say they feel disappointed and upset when they negatively compare their looks to those of their peers. The physical changes that you go through as a teen, combined with wanting to feel accepted by friends, makes it understandable to worry about measuring up to the perceived attractiveness of your peers.

It can be easy to forget that not everyone grows or develops at the same pace or in the same way. Comparing yourself unfavorably to others takes you on a trip to worry wasteland.

Even if you are not actively comparing yourself to others, comments and reactions from your friends and peers can have a lot of influence over how you feel about your own attractiveness. Friends may not realize how damaging their teasing and negative comments can be, but remarks that find fault with your appearance can be really hurtful. Even indirect, nonspecific comments such as "You look different" may feel very unsettling.

Teens like Tanya in the following story happily share with me feeling less worried, emotionally lighter, and happier when they learn to see both themselves and their peers in a more accepting, favorable way. Teens who have less judgment about their own looks compared to those of their peers learn to appreciate themselves more.

Tanya's Story

When she first came to me for counseling, Tanya, age fourteen, told me: "I hate how I look. I wish I looked like the popular girls in school that guys think are really hot." Tanya had become consumed with comparing her face and body to the "popular girls." She began eating less in order to lose weight, and she read tips online about how to get the perfect bikini body, hoping to compete with girls at school. One day Tanya came to see me with tears streaming down her face. She said she was miserable and wanted out of the peer-body-comparison trap. She then agreed to learn mindfulness to feel better about herself compared to her peers.

As a beginning step, I encouraged Tanya to see her physical self with far less negative judgment by anchoring herself in mindfully noticing the beauty of nature around her. In addition—perhaps you've heard of having an "attitude of gratitude"?—Tanya learned that an attitude of gratitude for her body helped to reduce her worrying about how it looked compared to her peers.

Following are two exercises that Tanya and other teens found helpful to manage urges to unfavorably compare their appearance to those of their peers. These are meant not as "quick fixes" but rather as ongoing practices for a more positive body image. Teens tell me that doing either or both of these exercises at least twice a week, for even five minutes, helps them feel less worried about body-image issues. The teens who strive to do these daily tell me they feel even more accepting and positive about their looks! As with the other exercises throughout this book, however, don't set yourself up to burn out or bail on them by forcing yourself to do them for a certain length of time or with a certain frequency.

this this! Seeing Yourself with "Nature Eyes"

When you see the world in a mindful way, you notice its beauty without making conscious comparisons. In just a few steps, you can begin to learn how to shift your thinking in this way.

1. Take a few calming, mindful breaths.

2. Imagine and reflect on a beautiful flower. Or search the web to find a picture of a flower, or situate yourself to look at a real flower.

3. Notice the flower on its own. Look at the uniqueness of its petals and how they are attached.

4. Notice the individual beauty of this flower. Yes, it may have some weeds surrounding it, yet it's pleasant to look at—there's just something about it that makes it special.

5. Now focus on a mental image of yourself surrounded by your peers.

6. Notice your own uniqueness and beauty. As you may recall from chapter 4, "Know your value" are three wonderful words that teens tell me helps them good about themselves. "Know your value" is a really helpful mantra that teens tell me empowers them to find the "good stuff" in their appearance. If you have been struggling with a negative body image and have a hard time seeing anything uniquely beautiful about yourself, then take another look at yourself through the same eyes that you used to see this image of a flower. Cherish the color of your eyes, your smile, your hair, your dimples, your jawline, or your cheekbones just as you did the parts of the flower.

7. Notice how freeing it feels to value yourself with the same "nature eyes" and not feel tied to how you look in comparison to others.

Remember RAIN (**R**ecognize, **A**llow, **I**nquire and investigate, **N**ot totally define yourself), from chapter 5? Focusing on her body-image worries, Tanya used RAIN to:

(R) Recognize her desire to compare herself physically to her peers. This included her thoughts of feeling inadequate and defective.

(A) Allow herself to notice these thoughts without trying to fight or suppress them. She accepted they were there in her mind.

(I) Inquire and investigate how these thoughts of negative comparison and inadequacy made her feel. In Tanya's case, this meant feeling inadequate and sad.

(N) Not totally define herself by asking: "Does comparing how I look to my peers have value to me? Do these thoughts and feelings have to define how I see myself, or can I embrace more positive thoughts and feelings about my appearance?"

Try it yourself to explore how you can manage your own tendencies to compare the way you look to the way your peers look.

try this! Washing Away Negative Comparisons with RAIN

(R) Recognize: Take a few deep breaths and reflect on how you feel when comparing your appearance to your peers. Does this make you feel stressed or feel better about yourself, or do you feel nothing at all?

(A) Allow: Accept these thoughts and feelings, and just allow them to be, without judging them.

(I) Inquire and Investigate: Ask yourself, how is comparing yourself to your peers helpful to your body image? How is it hurtful to your body image?

(N) Not Totally Defining Yourself: Notice yourself as distinct from your peers and having unique value for how you look. Can you see what you value regarding your body image as independent from how it stacks up compared to others?

Now let's discuss the impact of social media on teens' body image.

Images of Perfection in the Media

Our beauty-obsessed culture inundates us with images of music performers, movie stars, and models with seemingly flawless skin and six-pack abs, great figures, and perfect faces and hair. Teens have wistfully shown me social media images of celebrities and others whom they admire that get thousands of "likes." These teens tell me they yearn to look prettier, be more buff, or otherwise have perfect bodies so that they might get more "likes" themselves.

You likely know of celebrities, models, and movie stars who seem to look perfect—in an airbrushed, digitally altered kind of way. The huge temptation for both male and female teens to compare themselves to these "perfect bodies" in the general media and social media is understandable. Such comparisons with unrealistic images, however, usually lead teens to feel inadequate.

Teens in Their Own Words

"Social media and people I see in the movies is torture sometimes, because in the summer you see girls in bikinis with flat tummies and perfect bodies. You see people comment on social media about body goals, but you know in the back of your head that you will never meet those same goals."
—Marissa, age fourteen

"I feel so flabby when I look at the images online. When we had a team photo for soccer, I was cramping from flexing and holding it for the picture." —Tom, age fifteen

"Models have these perfect thigh gaps, and they are always showing them, and it's like if you don't have the thigh gap then there is something wrong with you." —Julie, age fifteen

"I think that social media is a big problem, because now our bodies are judged online in addition to being judged in person."
—Jen, age seventeen

"Body image is this perfect image in your head. I see those perfect images in the movies and websites, and you can never match that image in your head." —Manuel, age eighteen

We've discussed the power of acceptance as part of mindfulness throughout this book. When it comes to your body image, accepting that your body will probably not compete with airbrushed images of celebrities can actually give you a more empowered attitude to value and take care of it. The judgment-free zone that acceptance creates in your mind goes a long way toward reducing body-image worries. Check out how

Hannah learned to deal with her social media-driven body-image worries.

Hannah's Story

Hannah really loved social media. She would "like" photos of friends and celebrities who were really attractive, but comparing her body to these "perfect people" with great bodies made her insecure. Hannah gave compliments to her friends for achieving "body goals," telling them how they resembled certain celebrities. Desperately seeking a body resembling those she so deeply envied, she sought to lose weight. She started being very concerned about what she ate, and she felt anxious when on social media. She lost weight and became irritable because she was often hungry.

In counseling, Hannah learned to better appreciate and accept herself. One exercise we did was to focus on valuing herself from the inside out while reframing social media as a helpful channel for a positive body image. She learned to love herself without pressure to look like those people on social media.

Here is an exercise Hannah found helpful for feeling self-love and sending it out to share through social media.

try this! Going Viral with a Self-Acceptance Hug

1. Breathe in and out mindfully a few times.

    (You can do the following steps in your imagination or in reality.)

2.   Hug yourself.

3.   While hugging yourself, feel the warmth of your body and feel close to yourself in the here and now.

4.   If you can, take a picture or have someone take one of you hugging yourself.

5.   Post the photo or a written description about this experience on social media.

6.   Reflect on sending your message of self-acceptance and self-love to the rest of the world.

Afterward, ask yourself how it feels to appear (or imagine appearing) before others and sharing your self-love compared to letting online images rule over how you love yourself. How does self-acceptance of your physical self help you see positive qualities beyond your appearance?

Now that you've worked on your relationship with social media for a better body image, let's look at how your relationships with your family members can impact your body image as well.

Family Dynamics

What parents and other family members say and do can impact teens' body image in both positive and negative ways. On the positive side, teens tell me that when parents and siblings give them compliments and reassurance about how they look, it helps them feel better about their body image. Although teens may not outright admit appreciating this supportive feedback from family members, I hear from them that they value it.

At the same time, some teen clients of mine have shared instances in which family members negatively influenced their body image, whether intentionally or unintentionally. For example, one teenage girl frequently heard her mother complain about her own weight and body image. This drove the daughter to hold negative feelings about how she, herself, looked. Another female teen recalled to me her older brother telling her that she looked fat in her gymnastics leotard. She further struggled with frustration over her younger sister getting lots of attention as "the pretty one with the great body."

In short, indirect comparisons and rivalries with family members, or comments about body weight, how clothes fit, or other appearance-related subjects in family life, can feel very upsetting to teens. For example, Paul felt badly about his looks when comparing himself to his dad.

Paul's Story

When Paul, a high-school senior, came to see me one day, he looked depressed. He slumped in a chair and hung his head. Then he explained why he was feeling down in the dumps: "My dad thought he was funny when he snuck up on me the other day and jokingly made like he was going to punch me in the stomach. He told me I was getting soft. He didn't really hit me, but it really bothered me. Know what I'm sayin'?" When I asked Paul about being upset by this, he said, "Dr. Jeff, you've seen my dad. He's ridiculously jacked and ripped, and I am short and skinny. It's crazy, dude. Like, the girls in my grade even tell me my dad is hot. That's plain freakin' weird in my

*book. And, my dad is always telling me that I need to be in
good shape. That puts way too much pressure on me and gets
me really upset. For real, though, my dad's a stud, and I will
never be like him! It just really sucks for me!"*

*Paul eventually realized that striving to be a "stud" just
like his dad just made him feel like a dud and dislike himself.
One of the breakthroughs for Paul in our sessions was to
embrace an attitude of nonstriving when it came to seeing his
body. Nonstriving, in the true sense of mindfulness, refers to
accepting things the way they are and being in the moment to
experience them. For Paul, this meant learning to notice his
body without the rigid judgment that came with the pressure
he put on himself to compete with his dad.*

*To help Paul stop unfavorably comparing himself to his
father, he used the NOW mindfulness strategy discussed
earlier on.*

Here's how Paul used NOW to view what his dad's body
represented to him in a different way.

(N) Noticing his dad's broad shoulders as previously
distracting him by feeling inadequate about his own body,
Paul shifted to noticing feelings of pride, seeing his dad as
a strong father to admire.

(O) Observing both his prideful feelings toward his
father and his still remaining feelings of inadequacy, Paul
allowed himself to nonjudgmentally let these conflicting
feelings coexist.

(W) Willingly letting go of striving to compete with his
dad, Paul brought to mind aspects of his own strength he

valued, such as being captain of the debate team and being a friend others could trust. He also let go of using his dad's body as a yardstick for his own manliness.

If you have struggled with body image related to any kind of family dynamics or perceived pressures, the following exercise can help you get in touch with family-related body-image anxiety and let it go, NOW.

try this! NOW Letting Go of Body-Image-Related Family Baggage

Begin with a few mindful breaths, and reflect on how you have felt or feel about your body and appearance in relation to your family members.

- (N) Notice thoughts and images of how your relationship with your body and appearance in general has been influenced within your family.

- (O) Observe how these messages and images have either negatively impacted or positively supported your body image.

- (W) Willingly let in affirming feelings and let go of any thoughts or images that are painful.

Afterward, ask yourself whether you perceived any value in noticing the messages you get from your family about your appearance in relation to others. What body-image-related themes came to mind in considering how your family members relate to you and to one another?

Looking Your Best from the Inside Out

The chapter is almost over. At this point, you may be thinking, *So how I do this no-judgment, nonstriving mindfulness stuff and still take pride in my appearance?* The answer lies in remembering that mindfulness calms your reacting brain and stops you from setting unrealistic goals or getting super frustrated when trying to meet them. Although it may seem counterintuitive, it's important that you accept your body and appearance as they are before you take action to improve your physical self.

Let's say that you are trying to drop a few pounds and slim down, within reason. Staying mindful that it takes focus and effort will likely help you reach and maintain your weight-loss goal better than mindlessly and obsessively chasing after an unhealthy or unrealistic goal. Or, perhaps you want to change your hairstyle or dress differently? Knowing your value on the inside will help you value any changes you make on the outside.

With that said, here's a fail-safe, instant body-image picker-upper—maintaining good posture.

Slouching is a common teenage "affliction" that can leave you feeling tired and defeated. You may slouch because of body-image worries, but being mindful to straighten up with good strong posture can actually decrease those worries. That's because good posture helps you feel more confident. And others will see you as more confident in response to your more self-assured posture.

try this! Mindfully Positioning Yourself for Better Posture

1. Breathe in and out mindfully a few times.

2. Sit up or stand up, and looking at yourself in a full-length or large mirror, notice your posture. Are you leaning to the side, slumped, or sitting/standing straight?

3. Breathe in confidence, by imagining holding yourself straight and tall like a strong tree, and shift to sit up or stand up straight.

4. Hold this improved posture and reflect on how you feel. How does your body feel differently when you hold a confident posture? How do you feel emotionally?

Afterward, would you say that shifting to a better posture helped you feel more confident and relaxed?

In this chapter, you learned that mindfulness helps you notice your body in a less judgmental and more accepting way. Mindfulness moves your attention away from obsessing about how you look on the outside and helps you accept your body from the inside. It can also help you set healthier goals and feel better about any changes you make to your appearance. Maintaining a good posture helps support a healthy body image.

Check out what the following teens shared with me about how mindfulness helped them with their body image.

Teens in Their Own Words

"Going running used to suck for me, because all I would focus on was getting my thighs tighter and try to have a thigh gap. Now when I run and if I start to obsess on my body, I think about mindfully noticing cool nature stuff around me, like the trees and wildflowers." —Delores, age fourteen

"It still bothers me if my skin breaks out, but the deep breathing and letting-go images that I learned with mindfulness help me stop beating myself up about my acne." —Judah, age fifteen

"I still want my biceps to look fairly big, but since I started with mindfulness I am less self-absorbed. Taking some calming breaths gets me out of obsessing about my arms having to look huge." —Danny, age seventeen

"The gratitude that I feel from being mindful gets me feeling more positive about my body, because the more I appreciate being healthy and what I like about my looks, the less critical I am about my body in general." —Anna, age eighteen

Now that you have worked mindfully on your body image, let's put mindfulness to work to reduce tensions within your family.

chapter 9

freeing yourself from family frustrations

Family is not an important thing—it's everything.

—Michael J. Fox

Our families are generally important sources of love, joy, and support. Most teens express to me that they really do love their parents and siblings. Sometimes, however, family members can drive each other crazy. Annoying quirks and mannerisms, unwelcome comments or unsolicited advice, conflicts over possessions or personal space, and joking that goes too far are examples of those not-so-warm-and-cozy moments of family life. Despite the presence of intense feelings, conflicts, and drama between family members, most teens find humor in the suggestion that they can trade in their parents and siblings for new ones. But it is no laughing matter when family-related angst piles up.

In this chapter, you will learn mindfulness strategies for managing the emotions related to common family tensions and conflicts. We will focus on those annoying power struggles with parents and the seemingly endless turf wars and conflicts you may have with siblings. If you are an only child, we will briefly address common challenges in your situation as well. We will also take a look at stress and worries that come with parental separation or the loss of a loved one.

Conflicts with Your Parents for Independence

Teens, when expressing frustration about their parents to me, mostly complain about not getting enough trust and independence. Parents who are anxious about their teens' safety, their ability to succeed, or even just their growing up in general, may show it in the following ways:

- Raising their voices

- Giving upsetting, seemingly over-the-top consequences

- Asking too many questions about their teens' friends

- Looking way too often on the school website to check their teens' grades

- Imposing restrictive curfews that get in the way of their teens hanging out with friends

- Checking up on their teens too often by texting or calling

- Lectures, lectures, and, yep, more lectures

It probably feels upsetting when your parents behave in this way. Teens tell me how their concerned parents make them feel as if they are being "treated like a kid" and not allowed to do things they would like. Here is how some teens who felt "smothered" expressed their desire for space and freedom from their concerned parents.

Teens in Their Own Words

"My mom keeps threatening to take my phone away if I don't text her back right away. Like, if I am hanging out with my friends and I mean to text her back and forget, she spazzes out." —Sharon, age fourteen

"My parents freak out about stuff that's no big deal. It's like they think that if I don't remember to take out the trash or turn off the light, then how I will be a responsible, safe driver when I am sixteen? Seriously?" —Bart, age fifteen

"I am so frustrated with them. I can't wait to live on my own and have my freedom without my parents worrying and nagging me!" —Tori, age sixteen

"They act like I am going to blow it and fail my senior year. That's nuts! There is no way I would fail out, but it is my senior year and I want to have some fun." —Ari, age eighteen

Perhaps you can identify with Sharon, Bart, Tori, or Ari. But, although it may feel as though your worried parents are the cause of all your frustrations, they probably have better things to do than "spy on" you. Try to remember that your parents have your best interests in mind; they want you to be safe and grow into a self-reliant, independent adult.

Beneath your parents' annoying, controlling actions is anxiety. This anxiety only goes to show they are human, just like you. I know that conflicts with your parents can be upsetting. But guess what? If you are willing to have some empathy and compassion for your parents' concerns, you will not feel so stressed out by them. And, to be fair, aren't there some times when your worries got the best of you, and maybe you've taken some stuff out on Mom or Dad? Certainly, from time to time, you "flip your lid" in family life, right?

The more you control your own reactivity when you're dealing with your parents, the calmer they will feel and be with you. Mindfulness can really help you keep your cool with your parents.

try this! Practicing Peaceful Feelings for Your Parents

When you're feeling upset about your parents' rules and restrictions, call on mindfulness to calm you. (An audio version of this exercise is available at http://www.newharbinger.com/39812.)

1. Take a few mindful breaths.

2. Focus your mind on your parents' love and caring intentions for you.

3. Breathe in, reflecting on their loving concern for you without judgment.

4. Breathe out any negative thoughts and feelings you have toward them for what they have done in the past or what they are doing now that bothers you.

5. Breathe in again, reflecting on their loving concern for you without judgment.

6. Breathe out, sending them peaceful feelings and gratitude for caring about you.

Repeat three times.

Afterward, reflect on what it was like to slow down and not think about your parents in such a reactive way. Were you able to see things more from their perspective? What are some ways that being less reactive with your emotions might actually result in you getting more freedom?

Okay, now that you have practiced mindfulness for calming yourself with your parents, let's move on to your pesky yet lovable (did I hear you groan?) siblings.

Staying Sane Through Sibling Struggles

As many teens tell me, life with siblings can be challenging and even super annoying. Competitiveness and outright jealousy over parents' time and attention can really lead to or heat up conflicts. Arguments and fights can also often be traced back to teasing that goes way too far.

If you're an older sibling, you may sometimes be astonished and frustrated at how much your younger brother or sister seems to get away with. If you're a younger sibling, you may worry over the difficulty of living up to your older sibling's accomplishments, or, alternatively, suffering as a result of his or her mistakes.

Here are some of the typical sibling hassles that my teen clients bring up to me:

- "Borrowing" things without permission

- Bothersome bathroom habits and messiness

- Television and gaming console time conflicts

- Hanging around too much when friends visit

- Not respecting privacy

- Car seating preferences or behaviors

Teens in Their Own Words

"My older brother hogs the bathroom and blow dries his hair forever. I really wish I had a secret formula to put in the shampoo bottle to make him bald!" —Gail, age thirteen

"I never know when drama will happen next with my older sister. She acts moody, and the only time she is nice to me is when her friends are over." —Brent, age fourteen

"My younger brother has ADHD and is constantly interrupting everyone in the family. He is super annoying, and I feel embarrassed by him with my friends and in public." —Carol, age fifteen

"My parents keep babying my younger brother. It's ridiculous how they shelter him. The way I see it, I have to toughen him up for high school." —John, age sixteen

---

Wouldn't it be nice to stop feeling as though your siblings are making you miserable? Well, with a little mindfulness, you can begin to let go of competitive turf wars and other ongoing struggles with your siblings. Yeah, the things they do will still bother you from time to time, but you can choose to be less reactive and not get so upset about it. Then you can get on with what you'd rather be doing instead of staying steamed at your brother or sister.

try this! Dropping Your Sibling Comparisons, Competitiveness, and Complaints

Here is an exercise to help you feel less stressed out with your sibs. This exercise can be practiced prior to triggering situations with a sibling such as the examples below in step 1. I also suggest practicing this exercise when you feel really jammed up with frustration or any other negative feelings about your siblings such as before you go to bed or in the morning right before you see their adorable faces.

1. Reflect on what you struggle over with your sibling(s). For example, maybe your older brother has a super-loud voice or stomps around as if he has lead feet. Or maybe your sister seems to live in the bathroom or goes crazy on the toilet paper or shampoo, leaving you none. Or how about those cereal-slurping younger sibs who drive you up the wall in the midst of morning madness?

2. Breathe in positive intention for a better sibling relationship.

3. Breathe out while visualizing your sibling frustrations as giant floats passing by in a parade.

189

4. Breathe in caring for a calmer, more connected sibling relationship.

5. Breathe out, visualizing each of your frustrations disappearing on the floats as the parade marches away into the distance.

Repeat three times.

Afterward, reflect on what it felt like to release tensions with your sibling(s) with this visualization. How do you think your siblings will likely feel and respond to you if you are calmer, more accepting, and less competitive toward them?

If you are an only child or want to understand some of the struggles of only children, check out the next section.

The Challenges of Being an Only Child

Only children often have relatively happy childhoods and usually turn into well-adjusted adults. As an only child, myself, I'd like to think I'm among the well-adjusted ones, even though I'm still waiting for my thinking brain to fully mature!

Only kids tend to have more opportunities for adult inter-action by being "the only kid in the house" to talk with parents and friends of parents. They also tend to be high achievers, because they're the only ones who can live up to their parents' expectations. Only children may also generally have higher self-esteem than kids with siblings because of the exclusive atten-tion only children get from parents. That said, only children may, at times, experience this concentrated parental attention as smothering.

And, if you are an only child, people may assume that you are spoiled, bossy, selfish, and dependent. This is based on a negative stereotype. As an only child, it can be really frustrating to have people think this way about you.

One of my only child clients, Liam, age thirteen, told me about a time he was at a friend's house and his friend's dad asked Liam whether he had siblings. Liam politely replied, "No, I am an only child." The father then remarked, "Wow, dude, you don't act like an only child!" This remark really upset Liam. To him, it was an example of the negative assumptions people make about only children: they assume that they're spoiled, they're rigid, they're selfish, and they're accustomed to getting all the attention.

If you're an only child, have you ever been told how great you have it because you don't have to share things with siblings? Yet you might actually value sharing things at times. People may think you're lucky to not have siblings intruding on your personal space; yet being an only child might feel a bit lonely at times. And, when there's a mess, wouldn't it be great to be able to blame a sibling, so that you don't have to be the one in the hot seat all the time? Perhaps you're sick of being told by jealous friends how great it must be to have your parents' attention all to yourself, as though the time you spend with your parents is filled with nothing but happy moments.

My point is that although being an only child has its perks, it comes with some common frustrations. Check out the following quotes from teens without siblings.

Teens in Their Own Words

"I'm jealous of my friends who, when there's a mess or something gets broken, can blame it on their brother or sister."
—Richie, age fourteen

"It's annoying not having another kid to hang out with when we go on vacation, so I really like when my parents let me bring a friend." —Grace, age fifteen

"Often people assume I am spoiled because I am an only child, and that gets really annoying." —Taylor, age sixteen

"I often feel pressure from my parents to be the best at everything and feel 'under the microscope' because of the stress of being an only child." —Andy, age eighteen

If you can relate to any of the challenges these teens describe, the following exercise may help you begin to see things in a different way.

try this! Accepting Your Only Child Gifts and Challenges

1. Breathe in, and, as you do, visualize what you value about being an only child, such as perhaps abundant attention from your parents.

2. Breathe out, letting go of the parts of being an only child that bother you.

3. Breathe in, seeing your friends, relatives, and others you feel close to who fill your needs for social connections and friendship.

4. Breathe out, letting go of feelings related to loneliness or negative judgment by others.

5. Breathe in, filling your body with waves of contentment and fulfillment.

Afterward, reflect on any insights about being an only child that came to you during this exercise. Did taking stock of your positive and negative experiences as an only child help you learn anything new about yourself?

Now let's discuss something that can be hard on all families, whether large or small: divorce. If your parents have not divorced, this section can help you get a sense of the challenges and struggles of any of your friends whose parents are divorcing or have divorced. Divorce can feel particularly scary and overwhelming for teens, but mindfulness can help ease transitions and promote flexibility for meeting the challenges of living in a family of divorce. For simplicity, in the following discussion, we'll use the term "divorce" to include separation for those who were never married.

Dealing with Feelings Related to Divorce

If your parents are divorced or going through divorce, you may feel certain pressures and worries as a result of your parents being apart. Teens with divorced or divorcing parents share worries with me about having both parents arguing at a sports or music function, about changes in the custody schedule that could impact their ability to see friends, and about not getting along with their parent's new partner.

To be fair, I have seen some divorces that involved only relatively smooth transitions. Some divorcing parents support one another through healthy co-parenting, which helps their children adjust to their new lives. Even in the midst of significant divorce-related stress, some teens seem better able than others to negotiate not only the normal challenges that arise when a family goes through divorce, but also unforeseen and sudden challenges.

At the same time, many teens tell me that they wish they could prevent their parents from divorcing, or, worse, that they feel as if the divorce is their fault. Others have high anxiety because they often end up in the middle of conflicts between their parents, where they struggle to keep both parents happy. They may feel pressure to "side" with one parent and to trash-talk, lie about, or even spy on the other. In many cases, teens have expressed to me that going back and forth between two homes is stressful in itself. Blended family issues are something I often hear about as well. Here is what some teens had to say about divorce-related stress.

Teens in Their Own Words

"My stepsister is mean and just ignores me. I wish things were back to normal, with just my mom and my little brother living with me." —Bruce, age thirteen

"I am sick of being in the middle. My parents act like they are in middle school by behaving the way they do." —Kelly, age fourteen

"My mom really trashes my dad all the time, [and] my dad says Mom takes all the money. It's all ridiculously confusing and hard to listen to." —Brad, age fifteen

"I guess it was probably best for them to get a divorce, but I am the one suffering the most. Like, my mom is really preoccupied with dating, and my dad buries himself in work for his job." —Paulina, age sixteen

"My parents get along really well. It's crazy, because while I don't want to see them fighting, it's confusing because sometimes I wonder why they even got divorced." —Curtis, age seventeen

Using mindfulness skills to manage the stresses of divorce, as in the following exercise, helps many teens I work with feel less stressed out.

try this! Letting Go of Divorce Pain with RAIN

Breathe in and out mindfully a few times. Then step into the RAIN:

- (R) Recognize the thoughts and feelings you have related to your parents' divorce. Are they mostly negative, or are there some positive ones such as realizing that you don't have to hear your parents quarreling under the same roof anymore, or having some new opportunities for alone time with each of your parents?

- (A) Allow those feelings to be present. Don't try to fight or suppress them, but accept them as they are.

- (I) Inquire and investigate how these thoughts and feelings have shaped the way you experience your parents' divorce. Has the divorce created changes that are hard to accept? Have any of the transitions due to the divorce been easier than you thought they would be?

- (N) Not totally defining yourself. Ask yourself: *Do these thoughts and feelings about my parents' divorce have to define me, or can they just be part of me? Are there empowering ways to define myself outside of my parents' divorce?* It may, for example, feel good to reflect on your love for each of your parents, realizing that you may express it differently to each one. Or, perhaps you can think about your extended family on either or both sides being consistently in your life as a way to strengthen your sense of family and ease any negative feelings due to changes in your immediate family. You can also remind yourself that even though your family is divorced, it is still, and will always be, *your* family. Be mindful, as well, that you are not alone: many other kids have survived and thrived even though their parents divorced.

Afterward, ask yourself how it felt to notice your parents' divorce in a mindful way. How can mindfully reflecting on their divorce help you see it in a less upsetting way?

Now that we have discussed managing stresses that come with divorce, let's address some considerations for helping you get through the difficulty of losing a parent or other loved one, should that ever happen.

Letting Go of the Pain of Loss of a Loved One

Over the years, I have seen some teens struggle with the loss of a parent, a sibling, a grandparent, an aunt, or an uncle, and, in some rare occasions, peers. It seems hard for teens to share their feelings about death. Sometimes they try to make it seem like less of a big deal than it really is, because it can be scary and overwhelming to discuss. Most teens are relieved to know that there is no "right" way to grieve. In fact, just knowing it is okay to grieve and to let go of "having to be strong" seems to help them accept and explore their grief-related feelings.

If you have lost a loved one, or if you know someone who has, it is important to realize that feeling sad, scared, or lonely is a normal reaction to loss. It is also helpful to know that although crying is a normal response to the sadness of loss, not crying is okay too. If you don't cry, you may have other ways of showing your reactions to loss, such as wanting to be alone, feeling irritable, or even feeling a sense of relief (such as if the deceased person was suffering from a painful illness).

Trying to ignore the pain of loss, however, will not make it go away. In fact, turning away from your feelings can make you feel worse in the long run. Some teens have shared with me unsettling dreams that I helped them realize were related to their avoidance of grieving.

Different people mourn in different ways. Consistent with the nonjudgmental theme of mindfulness, there is no "right" way of reacting for someone dealing with a loss. You can choose to grieve in whatever way feels natural or fitting to you. If you have lost a loved one, even if it was long ago, check out the activity below to open yourself up to grieving.

try this! Opening Yourself Up to Grieving

1. Take a few gentle mindful breaths.

2. Breathe out, releasing feelings of discomfort or fear of grieving.

3. Breathe in positive energy. It may help to imagine your loved one smiling, or watching her or him doing something that gives you a warm feeling, while reflecting on the positive influence your loved one had on you.

4. Breathe out, releasing any pressure to feel a certain way to grieve.

5. Breathe in, and reflect with gratitude on what you learned and treasure from this special person.

Repeat, if you desire.

Afterward, reflect on what this exercise helped you realize about the person you lost. What did you learn about yourself in relation to this loss? Have you made peace with what happened, or is there still more to understand about how it impacted you?

A Final Mindfulness Exercise for Family Struggles

I want to give you one more exercise as a stopgap measure to cope with any of the family stresses we have discussed. The following exercise, called Square Breathing, is popular in many forms among teachers of mindfulness. I have adapted it here as another form of mindful breathing.

try this! Softening Sharp Family Corners with Square Breathing

Reflect on current tensions or conflicts in your family as you visualize each corner of a square floating in front of you. If you currently feel no stress with any of your family members, then do the following exercise by applying it to past tensions or conflicts or ones that could re-occur or arise in the future. Think about trying, for example, to stay calm when Dad is also trying to keep his cool sitting next to you in the car as you are learning to drive. Or how about when you're trying to be understanding and patient when Mom is asking you for details about who will be at that party you want to go to?

1. Close your eyes and imagine a square in front of you, at eye level.

2. Breathe in, seeing a frustration with someone in your family, or your family as a whole, as one corner of the square.

3. Breathe out, letting go of that frustration and visualizing that corner as now softly curved.

4. Breathe in again, visualizing a second source of family stress as another corner of the square. If no more past, current, or future conflicts come to mind, then simply visualize softening this next corner as an act of sending warm, caring energy to a member of your family or even extended family.

5. Breathe out gently, visualizing this corner as softer, as well.

Repeat this two more times to visualize and soften the two other corners of the square. As you complete this exercise to soften family tensions, notice any added positive feelings by reflecting on the positive aspects of your family.

Afterward, ask yourself whether this exercise felt helpful. Can you see value in noticing family conflicts in a different way by visualizing them as softer around the edges? Can noticing the things that go well in your family further strengthen these relationships, routines, and patterns of valued interactions?

Your relationship with your family is a lifelong journey that takes ongoing patience and understanding. Mindfulness can help make family-related challenges easier to accept and navigate. In this chapter, we discussed how varying sources of family conflicts and tensions can trigger anxiety in your reacting brain. We reviewed mindfulness strategies to help you cope as different types of family issues come up. In the next chapter, we will discuss a few strategies to help you stay on a mindful path for the rest of your life.

PART 3

Staying Mindful for Life

chapter 10

managing worries for life with mindfulness

Practice is the best of all instructors.

—Publilius Syrus

Let me give you a virtual high five for making it to the end of this book. You have learned many valuable skills to manage your worries through mindfulness. A huge number of teens struggle with worries, and those who practice these mindfulness skills feel calmer and happier.

We have discussed where worries come from and what mindfulness is. You've learned how to use mindfulness for worries about school, in social situations and relationship challenges, to help you with your body image, and in family life. Remember, your goal is not to stop worrying. With all the thoughts that buzz around our brains, we all end up in worry wasteland from time to time. But you can use the quick and easy mindfulness coping skills you've learned in this book, along with some cognitive-behavioral therapy skills that were sprinkled in, to worry less intensely and less often.

This final chapter will briefly discuss some closing considerations for making mindfulness part of your life from now on. These include the valuable role of practice, being understanding with yourself when you do not practice mindfulness, using your digital devices to assist your mindfulness practice, and inspiring mindfulness in others.

Practicing Mindfulness Keeps You Mindful

If you took a shower this morning or last night (hopefully you did, for the sake of those who sit close to you), you know first-hand that there is a time limit on the "clean you" that emerges from the shower. By tomorrow morning, or probably sooner if you've exercised, you will need another shower so that you don't start to smell. The repetition to maintain good hygiene is similar to the need to keep practicing mindfulness to keep benefiting from it.

As another example of the benefit of practicing mindfulness on a regular basis, imagine a grassy field. For years you've been walking through that field by a certain route, and your footsteps have worn a path—the path of worrying. If you repeatedly walk through that field by a different route, you will eventually create a new path. Going a new way may feel strange and seem slow and tedious at first, when the old path is still faster and easier. But, as you use it less and less, that old, familiar path will start to become overgrown. Now imagine some wandering travelers happen upon the field. Which path are they likely to use to cross it? Similarly, by consistently practicing mindfulness you can carve out a new neural pathway in your brain so that your automatic thoughts—wandering travelers, in this analogy—go down the path of worrying less often.

It's true—with repetition, you can change the way you think. When you don't use it as much, the worrying part of your brain will become less active.

As you may recall, you can practice mindfulness on both an informal and formal basis. Taking time to look up at the clouds as they pass by, feeling the water from a shower on your body, experiencing the joy of playing with your pet, feeling the breeze on your face, and noticing your feet on the ground as you walk are all examples of informally practicing mindfulness.

The formal practices you took for a test drive throughout this book will also serve you well, especially if you make them part of your daily life. Most of these take just a few minutes to do.

You now know many skills, including mindful breathing, noticing your senses, visualizations for letting go of worries, scanning your body, NOW, and RAIN. Mindfulness gives you that gentle pause to clear your head, settle your mind, and also use the cognitive-behavioral therapy skills we introduced in chapter 4 to call upon your healthy thoughts to dispute and replace those unhealthy ones.

Teens tell me that creating "mindfulness reminder zones" helps cue them to take a few mindful breaths or do other mindfulness activities. See whether you can make it a habit to practice mindfulness whenever you set down your phone, sit down at your desk at school or home, finish working out or another activity, or walk through your front door. Your brain will come to associate doing these things with being mindful, so that you'll find yourself being automatically more mindful and less worried after you do them.

Taking time to be mindful just a few times per week can really help you feel less worried and less stressed out. The longer and more often you practice mindfulness, of course, the less anxious and happier you will feel.

Mindfulness Will Always Welcome You Back

Although regularly practicing mindfulness is important, I encourage you to manage your expectations. Yes, it would be great for all of us to breathe mindfully most of the day, walk mindfully every place we go, and visualize each worry passing us by as it pops up. But our daily lives are filled with distractions and time pressures that make it easy for anyone to get swept into stress and worries and lose sight of mindfulness.

When you drift away from being mindful in your daily life, remember that the nonjudgmental, nurturing spirit of mindfulness will warmly welcome you back. If you fall into the trap of thinking *I just can't be mindful, I tried it and it does not work for me*, or *I wish I could stick with it, but I can't*, remember that acceptance of these thoughts and feelings is the best way to manage them. This is because, as we discussed in chapter 4, a huge part of acceptance is realizing that at times you will struggle to be mindful. So when your worries totally get the best of you and you start thinking *Nothing can help me*, remember that mindfulness is as close at hand as your next breath. Teens tell me that seeing mindfulness as something that is always there for them instead of something that they "should do" or "have to do" helps them keep motivated to practice.

That said, let's now discuss a big challenge to staying mindful: living in a world immersed in digital devices.

Staying Mindful in a World of Digital Devices

The digital world is filled with absorbing and soothing distractions, making it challenging to mindfully tune in to ourselves and others. Remember, though, that the exercises in this book do not require much time. So you really can put down those screens for brief (or longer, if you are willing) periods and take some mindfulness breaks to calm and recharge your highly stimulated mind.

If you don't like to put those digital devices too far out of reach, guess what? I have some good news! Believe it or not, the digital screen world can be a great facilitator and means of engaging in the world of mindfulness. Here are some ways you can turn your electronics from hindrances into helpers:

- Use texting, Snapchat, Instagram, WhatsApp, Facebook, Tumblr, Twitter, Reddit, or any other social media platform to capture cool pictures of nature scenes and share or post them. One teen client of mine posted a short, humorous video of her dog licking her face. That experience certainly mindfully engaged all of her senses, which she described enthusiastically in a text caption.

- Check out the growing number of YouTube videos that provide mindfulness exercises and activities. Search for "mindful breathing" or "mindfulness meditation," and you'll probably find breathing exercises, visualizations and soothing sounds, yoga activities, and guided meditations.

- Explore the expanding world of mindfulness apps to reinforce skills you have learned in this book and to learn new ones. There are some wonderful gratitude apps, breathing apps, yoga apps, and meditation apps. *Breathe2Relax, Calm, Insight Timer,* and *Smiling Mind* are some mindfulness apps my teen clients really like.

Inspiring Mindfulness in Others

What's really cool is the more you inspire others to be mindful, the more this will inspire you as well. Passing along what you value about informal mindfulness experiences to your friends and family members is another way to stay on a mindful path for the long run. Noticing and pointing out beautiful flowers, cloud formations, sunsets, snow-covered trees, smiles on the faces of cute little kids, and glimpses of wildlife can make for some nice moments of connection when you are hanging out with friends or family members or when going places with them.

Just as describing your favorite food to someone brings to mind how delicious it is, telling others about the benefits of formal mindfulness can reinforce them for you. Sharing any of the mindfulness exercises in this book or others you learn along the way can be a valuable gift for your friends or family members, one that truly keeps on giving. I am often amazed how it inspires me to keep treasuring mindfulness when teens tell me how mindfulness helps them worry less and be happier. Here is what some teens had to say about their own experiences of inspiring mindfulness in others.

Teens in Their Own Words

"My parents downloaded a deep-breathing app after they saw how it helped me be calmer." —Juanita, age thirteen

"My friend couldn't believe that I didn't freak out when his younger brother sat on and destroyed our bike jump. I told him I learned a way to breathe mindfully and not get so mad. He asked me to show him how I do it, and he thought it was really cool." —Justin, age fourteen

"It felt great for me to hear my friend tell me that she started practicing mindfulness after I told her how it helped me worry less often. She said it helped her do better in lacrosse, and I totally believe her." —Louisa, age fifteen

"I told my dad that mindfulness helps me realize that not every situation needs a reaction and it is easier sometimes to accept that people are going to do what they will do. My dad and I then went and signed up for a mindfulness course at the community center." —Dante, age sixteen

"It's weird, man. I just realized that getting uptight was getting me nowhere. When I started doing mindful breathing, and picturing relaxing images in my head, my friends noticed. At first they teased me a bit, but then they saw me being calmer. They asked me to show them more mindfulness stuff, and it felt really cool to help them." —Todd, age seventeen

So there you have it. Giving the gift of mindfulness can lead others to use it, and this can keep you inspired to stay on your own mindful path.

Some Final Words

Your life will continue to present you with challenges, and there will be ups and downs. By learning about mindfulness and practicing it, you will be better able to enjoy the good times, and you'll have super-effective ways to cope with worries and those downtimes, too. Feel proud of yourself for having the willingness to learn mindfulness and for giving yourself these super-important coping skills for life.

Any time you get really busy and overwhelmed, or majorly stressed out, mindfulness will always be there for you. Mindfulness will offer you comfort and a sense of security throughout your life. One of my teen clients described practicing mindfulness as like putting on a warm, comforting hoodie that just came out of the clothes dryer. Whether you want to hold on to that calming image or think about mindfulness in your own way, just know that it will always be as close as your next breath, what you notice within yourself, and what you sense around you.

Acknowledgments

My interest in mindfulness was sparked years ago, when I attended a retreat at the Maple Forest Monastery and learned to follow the practices of the renowned Buddhist monk and author Thich Nhat Hanh.

There are many inspiring mindfulness authors who influenced this book. They include Jon Kabat-Zinn, Jack Kornfield, Tara Brach, Shauna Shapiro, Daniel Goleman, Rick Hanson, Karen Bluth, Dan Harris, Daniel Siegel, Mark Epstein, Richard P. Brown, Amy Saltzman, Chris Willard, Gina Biegel, and Dzung X. Vo. I also learned valuable information and skills from Gina Biegel's professional teen mindfulness certification course and from an inspiring child and teen mindfulness training seminar by Rebecca Wing.

I am grateful to Wendy Millstine at New Harbinger Publications for encouraging me to write the proposal for this book and for pitching it. Thank you, too, Elizabeth Hollis Hansen, my acquisitions editor, for your assistance throughout this project. I am highly grateful for the many "spot on," constructive, developmental edits from the editorial staff at New Harbinger Publications, including Elizabeth Hollis Hansen, Vicraj Gill, and Nicola Skidmore. I also want to thank freelance editor and proofreader Will DeRooy for his superb copyediting of this book. Thanks as well to Amy Shoup, the art director at New

Harbinger Publications, for developing an appealing and catchy book cover.

My loving parents, Evelyn and Lou, have given me wonderful support throughout my life. My cousins Judith, Lillian, and Leah have always been there for me, so here's a shout-out to you and your families. I also value the encouragement given me by the family of my loving partner, Marina. This includes Arkady, Eugenia, Nellie, Matt, Becky, and Andy. And thanks to my fantastic friends Ralph, Tony, Ed, Ivan, and Jim, for being in my corner for so many years through challenging times.

Appendix

Getting Further Help

If your worrying does not seem to be improving, is getting worse, or is interfering with your daily life, then it may be time for you to ask your parents or caregiver about getting professional help. Do you struggle with any of the following?

- Suicidal thoughts

- Increasingly disruptive worries

- Sleep problems

- Self-harming behaviors

- Substance use problems

- Eating problems, such as bingeing or purging

- Crying more than usual

If so, please talk to your parents, your health care provider, a close relative, or your school counselor. Help is available. But if you have never had counseling before, seeking it out can feel scary. Knowing more about some of the types of helping professionals described below will hopefully ease your mind a bit. Any of these people may be able to address your anxiety or other emotional health concerns, but I recommend you start with your health care provider.

Your Pediatrician, Primary Care Physician, or Other Health Care Provider

If you have not recently had a medical checkup, it is important to make sure that you do not have any underlying medical concerns that may be worsening your anxiety or other upsetting emotions. Medical conditions such as allergies, gastrointestinal concerns, sleep problems, diabetes, thyroid problems, headaches, PANDAS (pediatric autoimmune neuropsychiatric disorders associated with streptococcal infections), and Lyme disease may present, in part, with anxiety-related symptoms. Once these concerns are ruled out, then your doctor or another qualified person, such as your school counselor, can refer you to a professional who holds a degree in mental health (such as a psychologist, social worker, licensed professional counselor, or psychiatrist). Following are brief descriptions of some of the types of professionals who can help you.

Psychologist

Psychologists (like I am) have a doctoral degree in psychology (PhD, PsyD, or EdD) and typically five to six years of postgraduate education and training. They specialize in emotionally based problems and helping people develop stronger coping skills. Still, it's important to choose a psychologist whose experience makes him or her a good fit for you. Ask your parents about the possibility of having your pediatrician, family doctor, or school counselor refer you to a qualified psychologist who has strong experience working with teens and families.

Licensed Professional Counselor

Licensed professional counselors are mental health service providers who work with individuals and families. They have a master's degree and are specifically trained to diagnose and treat mental and emotional disorders and to help with behavioral problems.

Clinical Social Worker

Clinical social workers may work for social service agencies and in medical and hospital settings. They also may work as private practice therapists who diagnose and treat individuals with emotional problems and psychological disorders.

Pastoral Counselor

A pastoral counselor is a minister, rabbi, imam, or other faith-based professional who has received training in psychology. Such individuals integrate their faith and spirituality with their counseling efforts.

Child and Adolescent Psychiatrist

A child and adolescent psychiatrist is a physician who specializes in the diagnosis and treatment of mental health disorders that affect children, adolescents, and their families. Child and adolescent psychiatrists have completed four years of medical school, at least three years of residency training in medicine, neurology, or general psychiatry with adults, and two years of additional training in psychiatric work with children, adolescents, and their families. This makes them the most highly qualified professionals regarding the medicine-related complexities of mental health. Some psychiatrists accept insurance plans, which can make it easier for families to afford this level of care—do some digging or ask around.

A Note About Psychiatric Medications

Psychiatrists, primary care physicians, and physician extenders (physician assistants and nurse practitioners) are the three types of professionals that can prescribe psychiatric medications. The use of medications should be carefully discussed with your health care provider, so that you know all the potential pros and cons. Other important measures that may be first considered are counseling, getting proper sleep and nutrition, mindfulness exercises, facing your fears, physical exercise, neurofeedback, and getting involved in new, healthy, pleasurable hobbies and activities.

Being properly informed about psychiatric medications by a qualified health care provider is important, because it is not completely understood how these medications may affect teens' brains and bodies over a long period. In addition, some teens have difficulty remembering to take medications on a consistent regular basis—in some instances, even with adult supervision—which reduces their effectiveness. Another concern, especially for stimulant medications prescribed for attention deficit/hyperactivity disorder (ADHD), is the possibility of these drugs being misused.

Importantly, though, medications can be beneficial for a wide range of challenging emotional health issues. For example, I have seen cases in which medications used to treat anxiety, depression, and ADHD, among other mental health concerns, have changed teens' lives for the better. There are times that medications can be of use in making counseling and mindfulness strategies even more effective. If you're wondering whether medication may be right for you, it is best to talk with a child and adolescent psychiatrist, because these professionals have the most experience with psychiatric medications for teens.

Resources

New Harbinger Publications' *Mindfulness for Teen Worry* web page

http://www.newharbinger.com/39812

This web page provides downloadable audio versions of the following exercises in the book:

1. Being Mindful by Noticing Your Breath (chapter 3)

2. Sending Your Inner Smile to Your Outer World (chapter 3)

3. Eating Mindfully (chapter 3)

4. Seeing Beyond the Pink Elephant (chapter 4)

5. Floating on a Soft, Fluffy White Cloud (chapter 4)

6. The Body Scan (chapter 5)

7. Floating School Worries Downstream (chapter 5)

8. Using NOW to Manage Distractions (chapter 5)

9. Practicing Peaceful Feelings for Your Parents (chapter 9)

My website

http://www.drjeffonline.com

Contains more information, strategies, videos, and resources for teens.

Further Reading

Jan C. Bays, *How to Train a Wild Elephant: And Other Adventures in Mindfulness* (Boulder, CO: Shambhala, 2011)

Karen Bluth, *The Self Compassion Workbook for Teens: Mindfulness and Compassion Skills to Overcome Self-Criticism and Embrace Who You Are* (Oakland, CA: New Harbinger Publications, 2017)

Gina M. Biegel, *The Stress Reduction Workbook for Teens: Mindfulness Skills to Help You Deal with Stress*, 2nd ed. (Oakland, CA: New Harbinger Publications, 2017)

Richard P. Brown and Patricia L. Gerbarg, *The Healing Power of the Breath: Simple Techniques to Reduce Stress and Anxiety, Enhance Concentration, and Balance Your Emotions* (Boulder, CO: Shambhala, 2012)

Debra Burdick, *Mindfulness Skills for Kids and Teens: A Workbook for Clinicians and Clients with 154 Tools, Techniques, Activities, and Worksheets* (Eau Claire, WI: PESI Publishing & Media; Workbook edition, 2014)

Amy Saltzman, *A Still Quiet Place for Teens: A Mindfulness Workbook to Ease Stress and Difficult Emotions* (Oakland, CA: New Harbinger Publications, 2016)

Lisa M. Schab, *The Anxiety Workbook for Teens: Activities to Help You Deal with Anxiety and Worry* (Oakland, CA: New Harbinger Publications, 2008)

Daniel J. Siegel, *Brainstorm: The Power and Purpose of the Teenage Brain* (New York: Penguin Group, 2014)

Dzung X. Vo, *The Mindful Teen: Powerful Skills to Help You Handle Stress One Moment at a Time* (Oakland, CA: New Harbinger Publications, 2015)

Christopher Willard, *Growing Up Mindful: Essential Practices to Help Children, Teens, and Families Find Balance, Calm, and Resilience* (Louisville, CO: Sounds True, 2016)

Christopher Willard, *Mindfulness for Teen Anxiety: A Workbook for Overcoming Anxiety at Home, at School, and Everywhere Else* (Oakland, CA: New Harbinger Publications, 2014)

References

Alidina, S., and J. J. Marshall. 2013. *Mindfulness Workbook for Dummies*. Hoboken, NJ: Wiley.

American Psychological Association Survey Shows Teen Stress Rivals That of Adults (press release). 2014. http://www.apa.org/news/press/releases/2014/02/teen-stress.aspx.

Bernstein, J. 2015. *Ten Days to a Less Defiant Child: The Breakthrough Program for Overcoming Your Child's Difficult Behavior*. 2nd ed. New York: Da Capo Lifelong Books.

Biegel, G. M., K. W. Brown, S. L. Shapiro, and C. M. Schubert. 2009. "Mindfulness-Based Stress Reduction for the Treatment of Adolescent Psychiatric Outpatients: A Randomized Clinical Trial." *Journal of Consulting and Clinical Psychology* 77: 855–66.

Brach, T. 2016. "Feeling Overwhelmed? Remember 'RAIN'." X, January 13. http://www.mindful.org/tara-brach-rain-mindfulness-practice.

Dr Daniel Siegel Presenting a Hand Model of the Brain (video). 2012. FtMyersFamPsych, February 29. https://www.youtube.com/watch?v=gm9CIJ74Oxw.

Georgetown University Medical Center. 2017. "Mindfulness Meditation Training Lowers Biomarkers of Stress in

Response to Anxiety Disorder." Science Daily, January 24. www.sciencedaily.com/releases/2017/01/170124111354.htm.

Hanson, R. 2013. *Hardwiring Happiness: The New Brain Science of Contentment, Calm, and Confidence.* New York: Harmony.

Nhat Hanh, Thich. 1992. *Peace Is Every Step: The Path of Mindfulness in Everyday Life.* New York: Bantam.

Salzman, J. B., and J. Salzman. 2015. *Just Breathe* (film). Mindful Schools, January 26. https://www.youtube.com/watch?v=RV A2N6tX2cg.

Shauna Shapiro: The IAA Model of Mindfulness (video). 2014. Greater Good Science Center, June 20. https://www.youtube .com/watch?v=JjeDjhFDRfI.

Tartakovsky, M. 2011. "4 Must-Do Mindfulness Exercises to Boost Your Body Image & Life." *Weightless* (blog), *Psych Central*, June 1. http://blogs.psychcentral.com/weightless /2011/06/4-must-do-mindfulness-exercises-to-boost-your -body-image-life.

Jeffrey Bernstein, PhD, is a psychologist with over thirty years' experience specializing in child, adolescent, couples, and family therapy. He holds a PhD in counseling psychology from the University at Albany, State University of New York, and completed his postdoctoral internship at the Center for Counseling and Psychological Services at the University of Pennsylvania. He has served as an expert advisor for *The Today Show, Court TV, CBS Eyewitness News, NBC 10 - Philadelphia,* and appeared on National Public Radio. He has authored five books, including *10 Days to a Less Defiant Child, 10 Days to Less Distracted Child, Liking the Child You Love, Why Can't You Read My Mind?,* and *Letting Go of Anger,* a card deck for teens.

More Instant Help Books for Teens

An Imprint of New Harbinger Publications

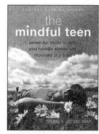